Reading the Water

READING
THE WATER:

*A Fly Fisher's Handbook for Finding
Trout in All Types of Water*

Dave Hughes

Stackpole Books

Published by
STACKPOLE BOOKS
Cameron and Kelker Streets
P.O. Box 1831
Harrisburg, PA 17105

Printed in the United States of America

10 9 8 7 6 5 4 3 2 1

Cover photograph by Jack Russell/*Fly Fisherman* magazine.

Library of Congress Cataloging-in-Publication Data

Hughes, Dave.
    Reading the water.

    Bibliography: p.
    Includes index.
    1. Trout fishing. 2. Fly fishing. I. Title.
SH687.H76   1988   799.1′755   88-2195
ISBN 0-8117-2263-5

To Jim Schollmeyer,
who knows how quietly a stream should be shared.

Contents

Introduction

Ten percent of the fishermen catch ninety percent of the fish. It's an old saying, and it's probably wrong, but it's not wrong enough. Fishermen who know how to read water, how to find fish, and how to present flies to them in a lifelike manner catch far more trout than those who fish the water at random. The reason is simple: *Ten percent of the water holds ninety percent of the fish.*

My brother Gene and I once floated a pristine stream with Montana guide Don Williams. I'd been having fair luck with wet flies, fishing them on cross-stream swings in long runs. We were anxious to cover some miles, but when we approached another good run I whined until Don brought the drift boat to ground. I hopped out and threw spray into the air in my eagerness to rush downstream, where the water looked best to me. I worked out line, began making my quartering casts, and gazed up at swallows swirling around the cliffs while I waited for something to rap my fly.

I fished two hundred feet of water before I felt a tap, then a strong tug, and a trout was on. Gene had waded in down below me and was fishing the same way I was, on my advice. He was a beginner in those days and often did what I told him to, though he's learned better since. I asked him to come up and take my camera; I wanted to get some pictures of this sixteen-inch trout, which was beginning to tire and dangle in the current downstream from the rod tip. It was a brown, nicely shaped and prettily spotted.

A minute later I released the trout and Gene handed the camera back. Just then we heard a shout. We looked upstream and there was Don, standing in a foot of water ten feet from the boat, playing a brown that was bigger than mine. But it wasn't much bigger, so I turned my back on him and returned to sweeping the run with a wet fly.

Gene didn't. He didn't know any better than to run up there to see what was going on. In no time I heard *him* shouting. I was expecting to have a fish hit at just that moment, so I ignored him and concentrated on the swing of my fly. A few minutes later no fish had hit, and Gene and Don were both shouting. So I gave up, reeled in, and jogged over to see what was going on.

It was pandemonius.

A long brisk riffle plunged whitely into the head of the run. Don had parked the boat right at the junction of the riffle and run. When Gene and I had scooted off downstream to fish wet flies he had watched us a while, then picked up a rod and lobbed a weighted Yuk Bug or Bitch Creek or some similar ugly nymph into the frothed water at the foot of the riffle. When the current delivered the nymph into the slower water at the head of the run a brown trout sprang on it. The cast was a long one, perhaps fifteen feet.

Gene joined Don, and on his advice made a similar cast. It had a similar result. Don released his first fish, made another cast, and that's when I heard them both shouting at once.

I took pictures while they played their trout, then each in turn while they held the fish. Don's went over two pounds, Gene's closer to three. I tucked the camera away, turned around to trot back to my own end of the run, but didn't get a dozen steps before Don shouted again. He'd merely dropped the fly off the end of the rod while he stripped out some line to make a real cast, but a fish boiled and hooked itself. I gave up and stayed there to take pictures. The two of them took about a dozen fish in the next half hour. The largest was just over three pounds. All held in a small bit of water over a seam in the bottom, marked by a slight darkening of the water on the surface. This holding lie was no more than twenty feet long, not wider than fifteen feet. Downstream from that the population thinned out into the kind that would let a fellow fish two hundred feet to take a single sixteen-inch trout.

When we were back in the boat, drifting again, I asked Don what had prompted him to pick up the rod and try that spot. "It looked like it might hold fish," he answered, which sounded like only part of the answer to me. Don took up a rod just half a dozen times on the five-day float. Every time he did he got into a pod of fish. I would have attributed it to day after day spent fishing the same water, but he hadn't floated that particular river in several years. He simply knew how to read water and find fish, no matter where he was.

Certain characteristics about that small piece of water hinted to Don that he would find fish there. The broad riffle upstream would deliver a richness of insects into the run below. The rough water at the head of the run would render trout invisible from above, safe from most predation. The slight darkness of the water indicated a seam in the bottom and deep water that would be a bit slower, giving trout shelter from a constant battle with pushy currents.

The place had all the signs of a prime lie. It was the ten percent of the water that held ninety percent of the fish in that stretch of river. I had galloped down to fish the other ninety percent, and from it had taken my share: the single fish that represented about ten percent of what we caught in that run before we launched the boat and drifted off to cover more miles.

If you learn to recognize the small percentage of water that holds the highest percentage of fish, you might not suddenly begin catching ninety percent of the trout, dazzling all your friends. But you are certain to begin catching more and often larger trout, which should be pleasing to yourself.

1

The Needs of Trout

Trout are like folks: they have a list of basic needs, they are most comfortable where those needs are met, and that's where you'll find them hanging out most of the time. *Reading water, simply defined, is learning to understand the anatomy of a trout stream so you can recognize the ways in which the different parts of the stream meet the different needs of trout.*

Each stream is unique; each has its own anatomy. A mountain creek, a meadow stream, and a large river all have separate prescriptions for filling the needs of trout. But there are repetitive themes from stream to stream, no matter what its size or character. Certain types of water occur within all the stream types and trout always hold where they do in accordance with the way moving water meets their needs.

A trout needs four things to ensure its survival: shelter from the constant force of the current, protection from predators, water in the right temperature range and containing sufficient oxygen, and adequate food.

SHELTER FROM CURRENTS

Shelter from fast currents is the first and most basic need of trout in moving water. H. B. N. Hynes, in his definitive *Ecology of Running Waters*, noted that, ". . . fishes are easily fatigued so even streamlined species which are well adapted to fast-flowing water cannot swim rapidly for long periods. The maximum speed of swimming of Kamloops trout in fact falls from 440 to 89 cm./sec. after only three minutes of continuous swimming, and all fishes spend most of their time resting in shelter." Trout would not last long facing the full force of brutal, or even brisk, currents because in order to stay where they were they would have to constantly swim upstream and quickly get tuckered out along the way.

This does not mean that trout will only be found where the current is nil. We've all seen fish feeding in fast water, and we've all caught them from riffles or runs where it was difficult to brace

ourselves against the force of the flow. In fact it is the movement of water that delivers food to fish. They need current, but they are most comfortable, and will usually hold, where the current is least.

The current is least wherever it is deflected. Even in the fastest water an obstruction will create a pocket of slow or still water. Many, though not all, of the tip-offs to good holding lies are visible breaks in the current: boulders, ledges, and logs are examples.

Not all of the factors that calm flowing waters and create holding lies are visible. The friction of a current moving over the bottom slows the water in a layer from a few millimeters to a few inches thick. The rougher the bottom the more friction it produces, and the more likely a trout will find a comfortable lie in the midst of water that seems too fast for it to survive.

Turbulence is another invisible factor. On the surface we notice eddies and swirls where water goes around midstream rocks. The same thing happens along the bottom, where the population of rocks is a lot more dense. Water flowing over a bouldered bottom gets into all kinds of conflicts with itself, one vigorous tendril of current canceling out the other. The result is a patchwork of quiet pockets, even in some of the fastest water.

The larger the rocks and boulders on the bottom, the more turbulence they cause, and the more holding water trout will find. Fortunately for fish, and for fishermen, the laws of hydraulics deposit the finest material in the slowest water, the largest material in tumbling water. The faster the water, the larger the rocks and boulders on the bottom, and the more likely there will be at least an occasional pocket where a trout can avoid the current.

There are quiet places where trout can rest even in the fastest water. But if all other factors were equal, they would seek sections of stream where the water was quietest.

All other factors are rarely equal.

PROTECTION FROM PREDATORS

The second need, protection from predators, is one of the primary factors that keeps trout from basking in the luxury of the easiest water. If trout always sought the quietest water they would also be exposed to the most predation.

Trout predators fall into three basic types: birds, animals, and anglers. Kingfishers are obvious along trout streams, but take mostly smaller trout and deserve a few in trade for their beauty. Mergansers travel in damnable family flocks, and are rapacious. On large rivers they are wonderful to watch, but when I see a half dozen of them scouring one of my small streams I have to remind myself that they are an elemental part of nature, that they've helped hone the trout into something that I love, that they're eating my fish but I am the one who belongs there least.

Herons can also be a factor on the smallest streams. When everything is in balance their predation is probably slight. But loggers stripped all the cover from the banks of a favorite local creek a few years ago. Since then I've seen at least one or two herons along its course in a day's fishing, though they were a rare sight before. Loggers killed the watershed, but I think herons fired the finishing shot; the creek is now almost barren of trout.

Osprey are the epitome of aerial predators on fish. But anyone who has had the fortune to watch one work, with its easy flight, plunging dive, detonating splash, and lumbering liftoff with the prey in its talons, would never begrudge one the fish it takes.

Otter and mink are the primary four-footed predators of fish, though I once saw a deer eat a trout and I've never been able to get anybody to do anything but laugh at the idea in the twenty years since that I've searched for someone to believe me. Otter are extremely effective. My wife and I watched a pair working an estuary once; they came up and crunched a small flounder after almost every dive. But that was an estuary, and those were flounders. I doubt if there are enough otter or mink hunting the edges of flowing water to be a devastating factor in many trout populations, not today. Perhaps it's unfortunate; I am delighted whenever I catch sight of an otter or mink looping along the shore.

Then there's us: you and me. It's our job, if we are to take them, to make ourselves seem the least like predators to trout.

Protection from predators can come from several sources. One of the best is water that is rough on top. Birds can't see through a broken surface to find fish. If they can't see them they can't capture them. So a fish under a foot of choppy water is a lot less nervous creature than a fish quivering over the bottom of a foot-deep glassy flat.

Shade makes excellent protection, especially when the day is bright. Contrast between dark and light makes it hard for the eye to perceive anything in shadows, unless the predator is in the shade with its prey. I once spotted a pod of trout working in eight inches of water on a Deschutes River flat. They were in the half-circle of shadow cast by a bankside alder tree, and I was out in the sun. The trout grubbed the bottom for nymphs; I would never have noticed them if one had not gotten overeager and broken the surface with its tail when it shot forward to grab a dislodged insect. That was its undoing; I caught it, and since in my youth I was a more voracious predator than I am now, I ate it.

Depth is the most obvious protection from predators. Darkness conceals trout. They feel the most security in deep pools and as a consequence are least wary there. But any water that is deeper than the water all around it attracts trout. A trench that is only two feet deep is the most likely place to find resting fish when it's located on a broad flat that is only a foot deep.

Camouflage serves as excellent protection for trout, and it is a form of concealment they use constantly. Their anatomy aids this adaptation: their bellies are light and blend with the sky; their backs are dark and spotted, blending perfectly against the bottom. I sat for lunch next to a favorite mountain creek one bright summer day. The sun slanted in, igniting a pool; I watched it for signs of fish, and finally spotted a couple hanging beneath an undercut boulder. Just before I got up to fish for them I scanned the tailout with my binoculars. There, not more than twenty feet from me, was the largest trout in the pool. It hung in the slightest gathering of the current, just above the pebbled bottom, its speckled back and sides glaringly exposed, yet nearly invisible. It did not move except to take an occasional insect, and it was not visible without binoculars except in the moments that it moved.

Trout colors change so they blend better with their environment. The change is slight, and not abrupt, but taken from darkness they will be dark, taken over lighter substrate they will be lighter. That is why a trout's beauty fades if you catch it and kill it: they are not so pretty dead because their colors slowly sink when life flows away from them.

Weeds are excellent concealment for fish, and offer protection from predators. Trout can rest among all the channels, down and out of sight. When feeding up above the weeds, all they've got to do is slip back into them when something like the shadow of a bird or the flash of a line sets off their alarms.

Ledges and rocks are perhaps the most common type of protection from predators in most trout streams. It is always a surprise to see how effectively trout can use the smallest of hiding places. They tuck themselves in when threat lurks and barely quiver a fin. They become extensions of this rock or that bit of ledge. They take similar hidden positions, even when not alarmed, from which they can safely survey a nurturing current.

When trout are alarmed, they flee at once to what the late Charlie Brooks, in *The Trout and the Stream*, called "bomb shelters." These are the deepest, darkest, and most remote parts of any piece of water. Trout bury themselves far back into crevices between bottom rocks, they sink to the bottom of the deepest pool, they burrow to the backs of undercuts that can reach surprising distances beneath root balls and banks.

TEMPERATURE AND OXYGEN

Temperature and oxygen, which satisfy the third need of trout, are two closely related factors. The colder the water, the more oxygen it entrains. High temperatures were once considered the primary factor in trout mortality during summer low-water conditions. But at high temperatures water holds less oxygen, and it is now thought that lack of oxygen, not high temperature, is most often the eventual and actual cause of death in these cases. The warmer the water, the faster the trout's metabolism and the more oxygen it requires. Ernest Schwiebert, in his thorough two-volume *Trout*, notes that ". . . fish require four times as much oxygen at seventy-five degrees as they need at only forty-odd degrees." These two factors, oxygen and water temperature, are inseparable.

Trout stream temperatures follow the mean daily atmospheric temperature by a few days: it takes water a bit longer to warm up. That is why trout do not perish in sudden but short heat waves. The mean temperature is approximately the average of the daily high and the nightly low; when you step into a trout stream to cool off on a hot day, you are enjoying some of last night's coolness that has not yet wicked off. Trout are saved by the same phenomenon.

Trout are active in water through the wide range from forty-five to sixty-five degrees. They will feed eagerly at temperatures of forty degrees and even below, but such activity hinges on the availability of food, and the insects, both aquatic and terrestrial, are not generally eager to be out at such low temperatures. A lot of trout activity is tied to insect activity. The aquatic insects begin to emerge when temperatures inch into the upper forties, and peak at temperatures between fifty and sixty degrees. Those are the temperatures at which trout are most active because that is when they have the most to be active about.

Trout begin to suffer discomfort in water a bit warmer than seventy degrees. Brook trout and cutthroat cannot survive much above the seventy-five degree range. Rainbow and brown trout can survive temperatures a few degrees higher, to a high of just over eighty degrees in rare circumstances where the water is highly charged with oxygen.

Sudden changes in temperature are most distressing to trout. Given time to adjust, they accommodate to normal seasonal high temperatures. But if the change is abrupt, mortality will occur at temperatures a few degrees lower.

At the opposite end of the thermometer, low temperatures decrease the metabolism of trout, nearly halting it when it gets within a few degrees of the freezing point. But running water does not freeze except in northern latitudes that are beyond the range of what we normally consider trout waters, and most trout will survive so long as the water does not freeze.

A rare season of anchor ice, forming on the bottom and working its way upward, can devastate running water. It kills aquatic nymphs and larvae; when it floats away from the bottom it lifts part of the streambed with it, tumbling it with the current to grind life to bits.

Whenever temperature and oxygen regimes approach uncomfortable zones, trout search for comfortable levels just as they search for relief from strong currents and protection from predators. The outlet of a cold spring might provide it in some cases.

The entrance of a fresh tributary often gathers trout in hot weather. In very short streamcourses, trout might move toward the headwaters seeking cooler water. In most cases they can do no more than move to where the water best suits their needs, which is why when temperatures are distressing you will find most trout in and around riffles and rapids that are charged with oxygen.

I once searched the course of a familiar stream for most of a scorched midsummer day. I couldn't find its fish. I'd been having luck there for weeks, drawing trout up to dry flies in all the long runs and slow pools. But they suddenly weren't where I normally found them.

I sat down to rest in the shade for a while in the afternoon, then got up to meander back downstream to the car. I tied on a wet fly to dabble here and there as I went. One of the places I absently tossed the fly was a short white rapid that fed into the choppy top end of a riffle. No fish had ever held there before. But this day a trout climbed on the first cast, and I caught two more there before moving on to the next white water. I landed half a dozen nice fish before I got back to the car and quit.

FOOD

The fourth basic need of trout – food – often overrides the other needs. Like the others, this need operates on some basic formulas. The first is this: *The energy gained from a bit of food must exceed the energy expended in the effort to acquire it.* If a large trout were to dash its bulk through several feet of water, battling current to do it, merely to take a #24 gnat, it would have lost calories, and therefore weight, in the bargain. This might be the sound basis for a diet, but it is well known that trout, lacking vanity, seldom glance into a mirror and gasp in fright because they're fat.

This rule of adequate return is obeyed more religiously as a trout gets larger. It is common to see a troutkin fling itself into the air after a small and elusive aerial caddis. You will rarely see a fish of any size make the same mistake. A small trout will sometimes hold in currents that are unlikely to deliver more food than will fuel its fight against them. It's a break-even deal; the

Richard Bunse on a flat in the Yellowstone River, just after a September snowstorm.

trout exists in equilibrium, without growing. Trout are like kids: if we could ever interview one it would probably fold its fins importantly and tell us that its greatest goal in life is to eat lots and grow up to be big and strong.

Truly large trout rarely move far for a single insect. But they do take up stations and feed rhythmically when a hatch is on and a little energy can be expended to take in a lot of bites, even very small ones. They will also chase a sculpin or baitfish down to its death, clear across the river, considering that the effort will be well rewarded if they manage to catch it.

Conservation of energy is the first rule of feeding fish. The second is this: *When food is abundant and easy to get, trout will often neglect the need for protection from predators.* During a fine hatch of insects, trout venture out and expose themselves to all sorts of danger, including that presented by you and me. They do this even at the price of a tithe of themselves. An example is the pods of trout that work the flats of famous spring creeks, at risk to both anglers and the occasional passing osprey. When a hatch is heavy enough they feed disdainfully almost at the angler's feet, turning up selective wet noses at all but the most exact imitations.

The larger the trout the more wary it will be. It is hard to say if a trout is wary because it is old or old because it is wary. But the largest fish are least likely to expose themselves to potential danger, and are most likely to be both cautious and superselective when they do. It is true that the biggest trout on the flats of famous waters like the Railroad Ranch stretch of The Henry's Fork of the Snake in Idaho, or the Letort in Pennsylvania, feed on small insects just like the rest of the trout. But they usually do it in the most difficult water, where they are protected by weed beds or fallen jack pines. And one must also consider that the very largest fish might leave the flats: trout are taken every year in the turbulent and canyoned water just above and below The Henry's Fork flats that outweigh their placid-water neighbors by three or four pounds. And there are rumors of browns on the Letort that hide most of the time and only come out to eat their neighbors.

TERRITORY

This subject of neighborliness brings up its opposite: the territorial instinct of trout. Fry and fingerlings hover in schools in still backwaters along the edges of moving water. But in running water they keep in contact with their brethren while aggressively defending their own bit of bottom within the school. As they grow larger their territories expand. As Schwiebert pointed out in *Trout*, "The prime fish will establish territoriality over the best hiding and feeding places." The biggest fish will be found in the best places. Reading water is a study in finding the best places.

Different trout species exhibit different degrees of aggression in establishing and defending their territories. Browns are most aggressive, rainbows next, cutthroats a bit meeker, and brookies often get chased into the neglected headwaters of their own native streams. These levels of aggression apply only where species overlap. The result can be that a smaller fish of one species displaces a larger fish of the other. But habitat preferences work into this equation, and it is doubtful that it is common, at least in natural situations, for a small brown to chase out a larger rainbow.

But there is less nature left than there used to be. Most streams have been planted – any stream that holds brown trout has been planted because brown trout are not native to this continent. So displacement becomes a factor. It is very distressing when hatchery trout are dumped into a stream that holds a good native population. Territory is piffle to hatchery fish. They are accustomed to holding ponds and constant fin-tip nearness of other trout. When a gob of them is injected into a stream they mill in confusion, and the result is confusion among the native trout that were already there. These unhappy fish can't drive out all the intruders, and they can't stand to share their territories. So they move out, leaving the field to the inferior fish. When displaced, native trout often die, which leaves one to wonder how planting fish in healthy streams can do anything but harm to our fishing.

Rivers get larger as they flow downstream, gathering more water to them. Trout drop downstream as they grow larger, seeking ever larger territories. According to Hynes in his *Ecology of Running Waters*, ". . . [trout] are limited at the downstream end only by the suitability of the available territories." That is why many trophies are caught in the downstream stretches of big rivers that are considered to be giving way from trout streams to warm-water fisheries, and also explains why an occasional lunker trout is taken by some barefoot innocent dangling a worm in a muddled river with the mere intention of catching some crappie or carp.

The best territories meet the most needs of the fish. W. B. Willers stated in *Trout Biology* that, "The territory is essentially a feeding area, and within it there is, according to most accounts, a single spot, the *station*, from which the territory is defended and feeding excursions are made." The station will be a place that offers shelter from currents, protection from predators, and a clear shot at food.

A trout spends most of its time within its territory, at its station, facing upstream. From this point it has a view of its estate. It can dash out to defend it from an intruder. It can nose out to accept a bit of food delivered to it by the current.

It is vital to note that the instinct to defend a territory exists only in running water. Willers notes that, ". . . strong territoriality . . . virtually disappears where there's no current. As water velocity decreases and finally approaches zero, mature fish begin to move about in a random way . . ."

Several interesting bits of trout behavior stem from territoriality. It's the reason you'll usually take the biggest fish first when fishing pocket water. The dominant trout defends the small window on the surface that makes its station the best lie. When something lands there it is the first to get there. If you learn to read the water right you can often pop your dry or plunk your nymph right to where the best fish lives.

Territoriality also explains why the fish you take from riffles are scattered across it. Each trout has established a small territory, usually with a station before or behind some small object that deflects the current. Unless these potential territories are frequent, trout will be sprinkled around a riffle like eggs on Easter morning. But move down to a relatively still flat, or into a pool, and the fish will be found working in pods. The water has slowed, their territorial instinct has decreased, and they're willing to gang up to feed on an insect hatch.

Territory is not a factor in bomb shelters; if trout can be said to worry, they are too worried about some outside danger, when crowded into a sanctuary, to worry about one another.

SPAWNING GRAVEL AND REARING HABITAT

Spawning gravel and rearing habitat are not survival needs for individual adult trout. But they are requirements for a self-sustaining trout *population*. Streams that lack sufficient natural spawning must be augmented by stocking if there is to be good fishing. This is especially tragic where man has caused damage to spawning beds in streams that have lots of feed for trout.

Absence of adequate recruitment can sometimes be detected by an unnatural lack of smaller trout. I had a favorite stream near home, in the coastal hills of Oregon. While I was away in the

Army, loggers sneaked into the watershed and knocked all the trees to the ground. The stream's spawning beds were destroyed. I had good fishing for the next couple of years, employing strict catch and release. But the numbers of fish in the four- to eight-inch range dwindled rapidly. Before long there were no fish left except a few ten-to-twelve-inchers—it was a very small stream and these were very big fish for it. Individual trout did remarkably; they were fat and well fed. But when they died off the stream also turned its belly to the sky; there were no smaller fish to move into its territories.

It was my home stream, and its loss propelled me to fish lots of other rivers. In order to catch fish in them I had to find out where the fish held. In order to do that I had to learn to read water.

Reading water is a matter of learning what is comfort to a trout, then discovering how the stream provides it to its fish. A trout is happy—if trout suffer happiness—when it has shelter from the current, protection from predators, and a temperature and oxygen regime in which it can thrive. It must have a territory that provides food sufficient for its size. A bomb shelter nearby will increase the value of a territory to a fish, and will help in attracting and keeping a larger trout present.

When a trout has found its ideal territory, it will be found most often holding on its station. It will maintain an upstream posture, from which it can survey its estate, defending it against intruders and picking off what food it offers. It will spend most of its time in a balance between holding and feeding. The key to finding trout is the ability to recognize lies where the stream makes them comfortable. The secret to catching larger trout is gathering the knowledge that helps you locate territories sufficient to attract them and keep them content.

2

Structure of a Stream

The structure of a stream dictates the way it will meet the needs of trout and is of more than minor interest to successful trout fishermen.

Running water is divided into a simple set of classifications. The water types are: riffles, runs, pools, flats, rapids, and cascades. That nearly translates into the way anglers think of rivers, though rapids and cascades are fishable only in pockets, and we tend to excise pocket water and consider it a water type on its own, ignoring the frothed and fishless water all around it.

One note belongs here at the beginning: though streams are divided simply into water types on paper, they are not so thoughtfully constructed when you go out and get wet in them. Riffles merge into runs, and the border between is usually, but not always, distinct. Runs flow into pools; exactly when they cease to be one and become the other isn't always clear. Flats are flats unless they are deep enough and fast enough to become slick-topped runs. But most of the water in a stream falls neatly into one of the classifications, and the water that doesn't is usually a brief gradient from one type to the other.

You will be fishing with certain tackle, and certain tactics, when you reach transitional water, and it's doubtful that you will want to gallop back to your car to trade your eight-foot rod for a nine-footer, your dry line for a wet-tip, and your dry fly for a weighted nymph just so you can fish a few feet of water that is no longer a riffle, but is not yet a run.

Keep doing what you were doing until it no longer works. Then figure out what to do based on what the new water type wants, where its fish hold, and how they are feeding – or not feeding.

WATER TYPES

Though they are further defined in later chapters, some early notes on water types will be helpful because the rest of this book is constructed around them.

Water type is a function of three things: the gradient, or rate of descent, of the stream bottom; the type of material that lies on the bottom; and the depth of the water that flows over it. Each water type has a different structure, and each structure pleases trout in a different way.

Riffles are stretches of stream that are cobbled on the bottom and shallow enough that this bumpiness is reflected up to the top. What you see when you approach one is a surface that is rippled or choppy, depending on the size of the stones on the bottom and the depth of the water between the bottom and top. Normally a riffle's rocks are softball-sized or smaller, its water three feet deep or shallower. The streambed is slightly tilted, so the water moves at an accelerated pace.

Some riffles are tipped so steep that the water rushes over them too fast and too thin to hold trout. These aren't worth fishing, but they are among the richest areas of any stream in terms of aquatic insect life. You will almost always find trout in the nearest holding water downstream, feeding greedily on insects delivered down the riffles.

Runs are moderate-to-deep water flowing evenly over bottoms that tend to larger rocks, bedrock and ledges, or sand and silt. The gradient is not so steep, the water is not in such a hurry, though it still flows forcefully. Typical trout runs are between three and six feet deep, though some are shallower, and are not defined as riffles because their bottoms are not cobbled and their surfaces are not choppy, and some are deeper and are not defined as pools because their depths and current speeds are relatively even from the head of the run to its end.

The surface of a run is often unbroken, but many runs that are three to five feet deep carry the choppiness of the riffle above them downstream throughout their entire length. Almost all runs display some unruliness where boulders break the surface, or where any kind of obstruction is so close to the surface that boils or swirls swim up to the top. But a run does not have the even cobbled bottom of a riffle, and its bottom structure will usually be reflected in a relatively calm surface with patches of broken water rather than the consistent chop of a riffle.

Pools are places where the streambed dips, then rises again. They are gouges or bowls cut into the bottom, and they are deeper than the water above and below them. Pools are the deepest parts of any stream, but depth is always relative to what's around it. A plunge pool in a mountain creek might be only three feet deep; a pool that punctuates a major river is more likely to be ten to fifteen feet deep.

A pool is a hesitation in the water's way toward the ocean. It is slow; sometimes it nearly stops. Where a current tongue enters at the head of a pool the water will be rough on top, and there will be eddies off to the sides. But the body and tailout of a pool will be smooth on the surface. The bottom tends to be the finest sediment in the stream, studded by large features such as boulders or even sunken logs.

Flats are about the same depth as riffles and shallow runs, but they are not so steep, their water not so fast, and their bottoms are composed of sand and silt or small pebbles and gravel. The smoothness of the bottom is reflected on the surface, which is typically slick. From a distance, flats appear to have absolutely even flows, but up close they often have mini-currents that push and pull a leader all around, causing drag on your dry fly that you will never notice and trout will never ignore.

The water in flats varies from a foot deep to about four or five, though that's a deep one. Because the current is slow, vegetation gets a chance to take root and weed beds become a major – almost a defining – feature of flats. Weed beds are rich in aquatic insects and flats are rich in trout, which often feed selectively on a specific stage of a single species. Flats can be the most challenging, the most damnably difficult, places to fish on any stream.

Pocket water is located in rapids and less often in cascades. Rapids are sudden steep tiltings of the streambed over bottoms of rock and boulders or ledge rock, creating turbulent white water. Cascades are rapids strung together, with a faster drop and a current that is usually too brutal for trout to survive except when passing through.

Pockets are created in fast water wherever an obstruction is large enough to cause the current to eddy in behind it. The eddy is relatively still; trout can hold there in comfort, with all their needs met. There is shelter from the current, protection from predators, and the constant delivery of food caught in the drift. The size of the pocket dictates the size of the territory and, therefore, the size of the fish that will hold in the pocket.

The last water type to be considered is that along the *banks.* This is separated out and given its own later chapter because a certain set of circumstances determine whether bank water will hold fish, and the criteria are the same whether it's the bank of a riffle, run, pool, or flat. Most streams have some fishable reaches of bank water, but most bank water along typical streams is low-percentage water. Learning to read it right will often put you onto trout other folks ignore and allow you to ignore a lot of water that other people fish fruitlessly.

STREAM TYPES

We all know what they mean, but still I'd like to define three words: creek, stream, and river. They all hinge on *stream,* because a stream, according to my old *Webster,* is any flow of water. A creek is a small stream, and a river is a stream larger than a creek. That's about all the dictionary gives us to go on. The cross references are confused a bit when the same dictionary also calls a stream "a small river."

We can work with this, but it will help to understand that a creek and a river are both correctly called streams: a creek is a small stream, a river a large one. When the word *stream* is used to describe the size of a piece of trout water, we can accept

Webster and use it to mean a small river, which I interpret to mean the typical medium-sized trout streams that most of us fish most of the time.

This might seem a tangle to you, but the result is simple and useful: a creek is small, a stream medium, and a river large. A *stream system* is the whole works, from the smallest headwater brook to where the water finally bows and exits into the ocean as a large river.

Water gathers in the hills and flows downstream. But a stream system constantly erodes its way upstream. This is a part of the wearing away of mountain ranges, a process one wouldn't want to stand around and watch happen. A stream system is a succession of stream types, from first-order headwaters too small to hold trout, through *mountain creeks*, to typical *trout streams,* on downstream to large *trout rivers.*

In a mountain creek, trout hold mostly in pools because every-

Jim Schollmeyer on a typical meadow-stream reach of river.

thing else is usually a rapid or a cascade. In trout streams, which have gathered from two to a few creeks to them, trout find the widest diversity of habitats: these streams display the classic riffle-run-pool structure that we all love to fish. In large trout rivers, good lies are farther apart and less well defined, but they are also likely to hold the largest trout. Eventually the system descends to the flat lowlands where it usually turns into a warm-water fishery.

Meadow streams, many of which arise as spring creeks, are variations in the simple succession of stream types outlined above. They range in size from tiny springheads that you can jump across to broad flats in large rivers, such as the famous Railroad Ranch mileage on The Henry's Fork of the Snake.

Tailwaters below manmade dams are another variation on the creek-stream-river succession. These are a relatively new type of fishery. Some of them are short-lived, depending on a set of circumstances that blooms, then bursts. But others, like the Lee's Ferry reach of the Colorado River below Glen Canyon Dam, seem to be lasting fisheries. Since some of the very finest trout fishing currently crops up below dams, they are worth a careful look in a later chapter.

Each of the water types and each of the stream types will be covered in separate chapters. But for now let's look at some features that affect all stream types.

Gradient is a measure of a stream's steepness. This in turn defines the kind of water it will offer its trout. As noted before, a stream system works its flatness, in geographic time, toward its headwaters. Its gradient is greatest at the highest end, less in the midreaches, least in the lower areas where it makes the transition from trout river to warm-water river. A stream's gradient is closely related to the geography of the land through which it flows. A creek plunging steeply down the slopes of a mountain is not at all like a sleepy river that drains prairie country.

When a stream drops with considerable speed it erodes its way to stone. The term *freestone* refers to any stream that has a typical riffle-run-pool structure and a bottom composed of rock. The faster a stream falls, the larger the material that forms its features. One of my favorite local creeks plunges over and around boulders that run from baseball-sized up to some you could park

Fishing a typical freestone stretch of stream.

a car in if they were garages. The average trout stream, lower down in a system, has a gentler gradient and a bottom composed of the widest variety of material, from sand, pebbles, and cobble, to rock, rubble, and scattered boulders. The lower reaches of rivers have the least drop, and accumulate the finest bottom materials. When a river has reached the point where its bottom is composed almost entirely of sand and silt, it is also generally beyond the point where it is considered favorable habitat by many trout.

Freestone streams have wide seasonal variations in their flows. In late winter and spring they are full and strong; they erode their banks far back. In summer and fall they drop, leaving substantial gravel bars along their edges.

Meadow streams, as opposed to freestone streams, have gentle gradients and tend to meander. Their bottoms are commonly composed of sand, silt, and pebbles, with weed beds common. Seasonal flows are reasonably stable. There is less erosion and the banks crowd in against the stream, often creating dark undercuts that make excellent lies for trout.

Neither rooted nor attached aquatic vegetation can get a firm grip on the bottom in strong currents. It does not survive in waters subject to winter and spring scour. It is characteristic of meadow streams and spring creeks and almost absent in all but the quietest reaches of freestone rivers. Because a dam tames a tailwater, and protects it from scour, a rich bloom of vegetation is generally one of the major reasons for the boom of such a fishery.

We tend to think of streams as either freestone or meadow types, wanting them, like we want most things, to fit into neat categories. But many streams are combinations, with some reaches of both freestone and meadow stream. The Gibbon River in Yellowstone Park is typical of this kind of structure, offering lots of excellent water of both types.

The terms *meadow stream* and *spring creek* do not mean the same thing, though most fishermen tend to mean the same thing when they use either term. A spring creek arises from springheads, but the resultant stream often flows in and out of both freestone and meadow reaches. On the other side of the coin, it is common for freestone rivers to surprise us with beautiful meadow-stream stretches. Few streams are all of one and none of the other.

STREAM ECOLOGY

The ecology of a watershed has everything to do with what kind of stream it holds. Timbered watersheds stabilize flows and regulate temperatures through shade and the constant release of cool groundwater. In most forested areas the trees along the edge of a stream are deciduous, enriching the water annually with leaf fall. Decomposing leaves become energy for bacteria, which become energy for insects, which become energy for trout.

Desert watersheds offer less defense for their streams. Their flows are marginally protected by narrow bands of vegetation in the river bottoms. But the upland area of a desert watershed releases water quickly. Overgrazing is almost universal now in sagebrush country, and the affinity of cattle for water has caused the river bottoms to be the first areas stripped. In typical desert streams today flows fluctuate widely and temperatures can be brutal, with punishing annual swings and abrupt daily swings.

Many streams have pastoral watersheds. These flow through farm country and are some of our most beautiful trout waters. The type of farming done, the way it is done, and the respect the landowners have for the streams all influence the condition of the water and the quality of the angling it offers.

The condition of a watershed directly determines the quality of the stream that drains it. Streams are affected by all things that happen on the land around them. In the forested Northwest, logging is the primary killer of streams. Carelessly done, it causes erosion, silting of the streambed, clogging of the spawning beds, and a reduction of insect populations that fish feed on.

Overgrazing on desert watersheds, cropping grasses down to the soil, limits the land's ability to impede the rush of water into the streambed after a cloudburst. Cattle trample and denude stream bottoms, limiting the streambed's chance of withstanding damage.

Mining is a less frequent problem, but a more damaging one wherever it occurs without thought for nearby streams. Chemical leachings from tailings, if they are not neutralized, sterilize streams, in some cases even painting them red.

In the industrialized eastern states the biggest problems are manufacturing plants in watersheds and development that sometimes almost displaces a stream. In some cases trout streams have been turned into channelized ditches. Trout fishermen generally view cement viaducts as poor watersheds, though politicians sometimes consider them causes for celebration.

Riparian zones, the narrow strips of watershed abutting streams, are being developed at a constantly increasing rate. Subdivisions and housing developments are crowding in wherever they can, to get a view of what will no longer be worth viewing when the subdivision is done.

WATER QUALITY

Water quality is a result of the things that have, or have not, been done to a watershed and the riparian zone. It is impossible to separate water quality from the quality of the watershed from which the stream arises.

Water chemistry is the first factor to consider in water quality. Running water is a richer environment than still water because the flow constantly delivers a fresh supply of nutrients to aquatic life. Chemicals that are the building blocks of life – nitrogen, calcium, carbon, oxygen, and trace elements – are suspended in the water and brought right to the plants.

Acidity is a major factor in a stream's ability to provide a trout fishery. The more acidic the water – the higher its pH – the less fertile it is. The lower the pH – basically the more calcium it contains – the richer it is. Rainwater and groundwater are more acidic than springwater, especially where the latter leaches through highly calcified soils. Spring creeks in limestone country carry the most usable nutrients for plant life, resulting in their richness in all the links of the food chain that lead to trout.

Pollution is a large factor in water quality. It is almost always a negative factor, but in rare cases it can enrich a river, causing plant life to flourish in what were previously less fertile waters. An example of this is the rich fishery that exists below Calgary on the Bow River in Alberta, while fishing in the miles of water above the city is relatively poor. The improvement in the fishery is based on the arrival of marginally treated sewage from Calgary.

Turbidity is a primary factor in water quality. Water that entrains a large load of silt impedes light, cuts down photosynthetic plant growth, and reduces the vegetative base on which the life of the stream thrives. Turbid water also deposits silt, clogging the bottom of the stream, limiting the available niches in which insects can live, and destroying gravel beds where trout can spawn.

The volume and consistency of water flow has a direct effect on trout fishing. Often the maximum life a stream will support is dictated by its minimum annual flow. It might be strong and vital for eleven months of the year, then suffer tepid low flow for a single month. All the life within the stream suffers, and its total trout population is limited to the number of trout it will support in the short low-water period. The limiting factor to life when water is low, which is usually during the hottest season of the year, is the twin killing combination of high temperatures and low oxygen levels.

Maximum flow can also be a problem on some streams. In watersheds that are logged or overgrazed, a storm and its consequent unchecked runoff can be fatal to life within the stream. Gravel and cobble shifts from one riffle to the next. Insect life gets ground up. Many trout are unable to find protection from the current and do not survive. Some trout will always survive, but in damaged watersheds the total number will not be what it was before the watershed was damaged, when the stream was protected from sudden high flows.

Artificial interruptions to stream flow can be just as damaging as either high or low flows. Dams are often the cause of both. They have several harmful effects. They halt migrations of spawning salmon, steelhead, and trout, a factor that has done considerable damage to fishing in the Northwest, where many of the greatest runs of fish have been destroyed forever by dams that cannot be passed to the spawning beds above them. Dams also obviously destroy the inundated stream mileage, turning it into lake.

Dams can sometimes be beneficial. The great tailwater fisheries springing up in recent years are evidence of this. The San Juan in New Mexico, the Bighorn in Montana, and the Green River in Utah are all prime examples. They are some of the best trout fishing in the world today, and the best of them arise from waters that were historically warm-water fisheries before the dams were built.

Dams that create tailwater trout fisheries release colder water from the bottom of the reservoir, reducing midsummer temperatures by several degrees. They act as silt traps and release clean water to the reaches below. They stabilize flows, reducing brutal spring runoff and increasing midsummer low flows to livable levels. They promote planktonic growth in the still water above the dam, which enriches the river below when it flows out of the dam; certain aquatic insects are able to capitalize on this new form of feed and their populations explode below dams, which can make trout fat and content.

The availability and activity of trout food always has a lot to do with where you will find trout and what they will be busy doing when you find them.

3

Trout Foods

I noted in the first chapter that the need to feed often overrides the other needs of trout. They will expose themselves to the force of the current, to danger, sometimes even to uncomfortable temperature and oxygen levels, in order to eat.

Trout move out of their territories to feed if a heavy hatch occurs in water where they would not normally hold. This is especially true on meadow-stream flats where the water is thin and protection slim. If enough insects get active there, which is a daily occurrence during the season on many rich spring creeks, trout routinely move out to feed on them, at substantial risk of predation and pressure from anglers. Of course they're wary when they do it.

A typical trout territory offers a compromise of the primary needs: shelter from the current, protection from predators, and food. The station within the territory is a specific spot in which the trout is protected, yet from which it can survey its territory to dash out for the tidbits a constant current delivers. When aquatic insects or other innocents get active, trout get excited. They leave their stations to dart here and there throughout the territory. If their victims are concentrated at one level, trout suspend themselves at that level and remain where they can feed with the least movement, the least effort.

Trout are most active when the organisms on which they feed are out and about. An actively feeding fish is more receptive to an artificial than is a snoozing fish, especially if the fly has some resemblance to the critter on which it already feeds. Because trout feed most often on aquatic insects, an understanding of the aquatics is essential if you hope to catch trout consistently.

I wrote about the aquatic insects of importance to anglers in *Handbook of Hatches* (Stackpole, 1987), the companion book to this one. That book tells you how to identify insects to a level that is useful, how to select fly patterns that match the naturals, and how to choose tactics that present the imitations to the trout as if the flies were the real thing. It is a thorough treatment of a subject that is vital to the angler and which I will introduce in this chapter.

Aquatic insects spend most of their life cycles under the water, as nymphs or larvae. This is the stage in which they do their eating and growing; it typically takes up about eleven months of an insect's one-year life span. But there are exceptions; some aquatic insects mature and emerge within a few weeks, others remain underwater for three or four years.

At maturity the insect emerges into its winged adult form. This is the stage in which it does its mating, egg-laying, and dying. This phase of life lasts anywhere from a few hours to a few weeks. The typical adult aquatic insect has only one thing on its mind—reproduction—and does very little feeding. The mayflies do not feed at all; they do not even have mouth parts or digestive tracts.

Mayflies historically are considered the most important aquatic insects to anglers. Part of this is because they are the most noticeable, and the prettiest. But another large part is due to their concentrated hatches, which cause trout to feed with abandon and with eyes that see no other critters.

Mayfly nymphs have adapted to different types of water. Slender and darting *swimmers* live in slow water; a few are found in riffles, but the most astonishing numbers thrive on flats where

Mayfly dun.

the current is peaceful and aquatic vegetation has taken root. They like to flit around in it, browsing on the stems and leaves of submerged plants. Robust *crawler* nymphs prefer faster water. They are found most often in riffles and runs, clambering among the cobble and stones. They have weightlifters' arms with which to hold on while they browse the thin layer of photosynthetic growth on bottom rocks. Flat *clingers* have the aerodynamics of an airplane's wing and live by clinging along the faces of rocks in the fastest riffles, rapids, and cascades. Like crawlers, they eat the same slippery layer of algae that we slip on and curse while wading. *Burrower* mayfly nymphs live in the slowest water, over sand, silt, or mud bottoms. Some wriggle into the substrate until only their eyes show, others dig U-shaped tunnels and live in them beneath the bottom, coming out to feed at night.

When it is mature, a mayfly nymph swims or floats to the

surface, where its skin splits along the back and the *dun* emerges. The dun has upright wings, a long slender body, and two or three long tails. They look like brave little sailboats adrift on water too big for them. As soon as their wings are dry, duns leave the water and fly to nearby vegetation, if they are not eaten by trout first. They tend to emerge in great numbers, in small spaces, and trout do their heaviest feeding when a hatch is happening.

There are three moments of vulnerability to the mayfly during a hatch: first, as the nymph makes its way to the surface; second, as it emerges through the surface film and the dun escapes the nymphal shuck; and third, as the dun rides the current, waiting for its wings to dry. The individual insect is largely helpless, entirely at the whim of the current and the trout. The survival of the species is dependent on the sheer mass of individuals that attempts to emerge, a few of which are bound to survive even in the most parsimonious times. This sort of survival tactic is a delight to feeding trout.

Duns that survive predation and escape to streamside vegetation cast a final thin skin and turn into *spinners,* the reproductive stage of the insect. Male spinners form swarms, often dancing in clouds above evening streams. When a female enters the cloud she is quickly coupled. Her eggs are fertilized in the air, then deposited onto the water. Female mayflies generally die spent upon the water; males may fall to the water or return to vegetation and die there, useless to trout.

Caddisflies live under water as wormlike larvae. They take one of two forms. Many are cased, carrying around homes of sand and pebbles, sticks and stones. These generally live in the slower water of runs, flats, and pools. Others are free-living, without cases. Some free-living larvae construct crude shelters into which they can retreat; others roam freely without any shelter at all. Free-living caddis larvae are most abundant in the fast water of riffles and brisk runs.

Caddis pass through a transitional pupal stage before becoming adults. When ready to pupate, a caddis larva either seals its existing case to bottom stones or constructs a case if it doesn't own one. The larval cycle lasts most of a year; the pupal stage lasts a few weeks. When the transformation is complete the adult caddis is wrapped lightly inside the pupal skin, which traps tiny bubbles of gas. It cuts out of the case and is buoyed to the surface by the trapped gases. In some species this float to the top is aided by a strong swimming motion. Other species merely rise at the whim of the water. In either case they are very vulnerable to feeding trout.

Caddis break through the surface quickly, cast the pupal skin, and fly off toward streamside vegetation in a hurry. They leave a lot of splashy rises in their wakes.

The moment of most vulnerability for an emerging caddis is the pupal trip to the top, especially in the instant before it reaches the surface to break through. When a caddis hatch is on, trout often leave their stations and hang suspended a foot or two beneath the surface, waiting to intercept helpless pupae.

Caddis adults have tentlike wings pitched over fat bulbous bodies. They mate in the leaves and grasses alongside the stream. Many species return to the water to lay their eggs by dancing and tapping their abdomens to it to wash off the egg clusters. But others actually dive down under the water, swim to the bottom, and deposit their eggs on bottom stones. The first group causes

Caddisfly.

excellent dry-fly fishing; the second group, once it is understood, can give you excellent wet-fly fishing.

Stoneflies have a simple life cycle: they live under water as nymphs, they crawl out of the water to emerge as adults. The nymphs thrive in water that is well oxygenated; they are found mostly in riffles and runs. Many are peaceful herbivores, browsing the thin layer of algae that coats almost all rocks in running water. Others are predaceous, prowling the crevices among bottom stones, hunting for mayfly nymphs, caddisfly larvae, and other innocent organisms.

Most stonefly nymphs crawl along the bottom to shore, when they reach maturity, and emergence takes place out of the water, safe from trout. This often happens at night. What most people think of as a stonefly hatch is actually the afternoon or evening return of females to lay their eggs. They hover over riffles or broad runs, helicoptering in to wash egg clusters into the water. This can be fatal behavior, especially when the insects are among the largest of stoneflies, therefore the most exciting to trout.

Midges are of questionable importance on most flowing water, but of definite importance in the slower stretches of streams. Populations can be extreme on meandering flats with silty bottoms and lots of rooted vegetation.

The midge life cycle is similar to that of the caddis: they live as larvae, are buoyed to the surface as pupae, emerge and deposit their eggs as adults. The wormish larvae are not of great interest to anglers, since they are generally tiny and not available to trout in concentrated numbers so that trout would be prompted to feed selectively on them. The pupae are extremely vulnerable as they kick feebly to the surface and hang suspended beneath the surface film. They are small, but so many are available that trout gobble them eagerly. They are the most important stage of the insect. Trout often feed selectively on midge pupae, rarely feed selectively on midge larvae or adults.

Other aquatic insects of occasional importance in running water include alderflies, hellgrammites, and water boatmen. Alderflies are caddis look-alikes that are more important on ponds and lakes than they are on streams. Hellgrammites are the larval stage of what will later become dobsonflies. They are very large and fierce; they will be happy to bite you if you give them the chance. They are primarily of interest to Midwestern small-mouth bass fishermen, and of very infrequent importance to trout fishermen. Waterboatmen are largely still-water insects, but they do live in slow, weedy water in streams, and trout do occasionally feed on them in such water.

Terrestrial insects can be of great importance to the trout-stream angler. Grasshoppers often find their way to the water. They get into most of their trouble with trout in hot weather, during July, August, and September on meadow streams. Grassy bankside vegetation that grows close to the stream favors the chances that they will get delivered to the water. Undercut banks and good holding water right along the edges promote the chance that a trout will be there, waiting for a fallen hopper. Timbered streams are less likely to be important grasshopper water.

Beetles, on the other hand, can be most important where a forested shore increases the chance that they will be blown out of trees in great numbers and wafted to the water. Other important terrestrials include ants and crickets, leafhoppers and inch-worms. Almost any insect, or even small land animal, that gets onto the water is fair game for fish if the victim is small enough and the trout large enough.

Baitfish, sculpins, and young-of-the-year trout are important food items for trout. The larger a trout gets the more attention it turns to these bigger bites, and the more it seeks the kind of territory that provides them.

Crustaceans are also important. Scuds are small shrimplike beasts that pedal furiously, upside down, through the weed-filled reaches of our slower rivers. They are comical creatures, but they are very abundant in favorable habitats, available all year around, and trout search for them hungrily whenever aquatic insects enjoy a day or a season off. Cress bugs, or water sow bugs, are important food on a few limestone spring creeks. They are most abundant where the water is rich in calcium, the flow choked with weeds. Crayfish are an obvious big bite for fish that live in large pools. Stomach samples reveal that they make up a substantial percentage of trout feed and that the larger the trout the higher percentage of crayfish it eats.

Leeches are largely still-water inhabitants, but they live in the slower stretches of streams. They make up a very small percent-

Stonefly.

age of the feed in a trout's diet, but fish seem to have a long memory for them. Any fly that imitates their sinuous snakelike swimming motion can draw a wallop out of a large trout.

In his Scientific Anglers videotape *Anatomy of a Trout Stream*, scientist and expert fly fisherman Rick Hafele emphasized that, "identifying the insect trout are feeding on, and its life stage, will determine at what water level you fish." Learning a little about all the trout foods will tell you what sort of imitation to choose and what tactic to present it with, as well as where to fish it in the stream.

The behavior of trout foods is one of the elemental keys to the behavior of trout. Learn what you can about them, observe what you can while on the water, and you will increase your ability to read water and find fish.

4

Trout Lies

Trout hold in four types of water. They are *sheltering lies, holding lies, feeding lies,* and *prime lies.* Each of the four types offers something different to the trout, and each satisfies the trout in a different way.

SHELTERING LIES

Sheltering lies are sanctuary water. They are what Charlie Brooks referred to when he used the term *bomb shelter.* They are where trout arrow off to when you approach a pool carelessly and see them scattering before you.

We normally think of a sheltering lie as the deepest part of a big pool, where fish cover their eyes with their fins and hide down in the darkness. But in a mountain creek a trout might dive under a log. In a meadow stream its sanctuary might be far back beneath an undercut, among tangled roots. In a spring creek the same trout might merely sink down to disappear among trailing weeds. On big rivers trout can usually find sanctuary just by moving a few feet out from the bank and dropping down to the bottom.

If trout have fled in fear into their sanctuary water, there will be little use fishing for them there. But if you approach a recognizable bomb shelter and it is undisturbed, you should consider it a holding lie and fish it carefully. The same water that provides haven for scattered small trout might provide a home for a single large one. After all, the old lunk will often get its groceries driven right to it.

HOLDING LIES

Holding lies are where trout are found most often. They offer some shelter from currents, some protection from predators, and a fair crack at feed: the kind of compromise that makes up most trout territories. These are the kinds of lies that trout spend most of their time in. They establish their territories, wait on their stations, and feed on whatever the current supplies them. Most of these lies offer less than perfect protection for the fish they hold. Studies have shown that shelter, not food, is most often the limiting factor in the suitability of a territory. The better the shelter the better the territory. The value of a holding lie is also increased by the nearness of a sheltering lie – a bomb shelter – where a trout can retreat in a hurry when its holding lie gets invaded by an osprey, otter, or angler.

Trout move through a succession of better holding territories as they grow larger. When they outgrow the territory they own at present they move out and dislodge a smaller trout from a better territory if they can. Another trout immediately takes over the old territory. Reshuffling is probably constant under the water as trout grow older and either move up to a larger territory or die trying, are captured by predators, or are caught and killed by fishermen.

Holding lies almost always have something to separate them from the water around them. It might be a rock in the current, a seam of deep water surrounded by shallow water, or an undercut where the water is deflected. Any feature that interrupts the current, in water that is deep enough to give even a slight sense of security, will attract trout. In general, the larger the interruption and the deeper the water, the larger the trout a holding lie will be able to brag about.

Holding lies always have something to distinguish them, from the trout's point of view, under the water. But the distinguishing features are not always visible from our point of view, above the water. Not all of the rocks and seams in a three-foot-deep riffle are reflected on its surface. The boulders that stud the bottom of a run sometimes cause boils on the surface. Sometimes they do not. Recall that a boulder the size of a basketball can make a pretty good lie for a sizable trout while never casting a hint of itself up to the surface.

Sometimes you must learn to recognize trout *water,* as opposed to trout *lies,* and fish all of the water as if it all were a lie. Trout water is distinguished by a nature that promises lots of hidden holding lies, but doesn't necessarily reveal them. Unfeatured riffles between two and three feet deep often fall into this category, with trout scattered across them in territorial niches that don't show on the choppy surface. Some runs that are three to six feet deep, unbroken on the surface, hold lots of trout without exposing the exact location of any of them. By setting up a searching pattern of casts that covers all of this kind of water, you will be sure to deliver your fly to trout that hold constant on their invisible stations, waiting for bits of feed to come to them.

FEEDING LIES

Feeding lies, as opposed to holding lies, are places where trout go to the food rather than wait for it to come to them. These lies offer lots of opportunity for the trout to get greedy, but usually don't offer much protection from predators. If they offered excellent protection, trout would hold in them all the time and they would be holding lies.

Feeding lies are usually areas of the stream that are rich in insects, offering prolific hatches. This kind of water is almost always shallow because the greatest amount of sunlight strikes the bottom where the water is shallowest: photosynthetic growth is greatest there, and the plant growth feeds aquatic insects. When fish move out of their normal holding lies to feed in such water they are vulnerable to predation – they know it, and they

Dr. Gene Hughes approaching a prime lie: a boulder in the "fifty-mile riffle" of the upper Madison River.

are usually wary. But if the hatch is heavy they sometimes concentrate so intently on feeding that they forget about raptors in the air, or anglers in the water.

PRIME LIES

Prime lies are points along the course of a stream where all of the needs of a trout are met in one place. These lies offer comfortable temperature and oxygen levels, easy living away from strong currents, protection from predators, and an abundant source of food. A trout holding in a prime lie does not ever need to move far to satisfy any of its needs.

The markings of a prime lie are usually visible on the surface of the stream. There is generally a steady current to deliver food, though in a pool it might be a ponderous current. The next sign is some significant break in the current. This can be a boulder, ledge, drop-off, or anything else that slows the current so a trout can hold comfortably. The final sign marking a prime lie is sufficient depth to give security from predation.

Where these three factors converge, you will usually find the largest trout in that section of stream. Recognizing a prime lie takes some practice, but when the factors causing it are considered, it becomes relatively easy.

Fishing prime lies is *not* always relatively easy. They are usually difficult. In fact, a fourth factor that points to a prime lie in heavily fished water is the degree of difficulty you must go through to fish it. The reason is simple: on waters with lots of angling pressure, anglers become the primary predator from which trout seek protection. That is why the fellow who is willing to struggle across to fish the stream from the wrong shore will often take the right fish. It is also why the guy who squirms his way into the most difficult indentation along a brushy bank often has the largest tales to tell of fish that got away.

Reading water is a matter of learning to read the stream's evidence of where trout would be. As Rick Hafele so aptly put it in *Anatomy of a Trout Stream,* "Learning to read water means being able to find where the trout's needs are being met by reading the *surface* of the water." You must learn to notice the indications on the surface that spell the different kinds of holding water underneath: sheltering lies, holding lies, feeding lies, and prime lies.

EMPTY WATER

There is another important kind of water that you should learn to recognize: water empty of trout. This is the largest percentage of any stream. Anybody who casts at random will employ his flies uselessly in this kind of water most of the time.

At the start of a five-day float trip in Montana, my brother Gene, new to fly fishing, cast to whatever water was in front of him on his side of the boat as we drifted downstream. Our guide, Don Williams, would call out, "Fish the other side," from time to time, and Gene would turn around and cast again to whatever water was in front of him.

But it wasn't long before Gene began to recognize which bank was best without being told. He would turn his back on flats that were inches deep to plunk a weighted nymph in tight against a bank that was three to four feet deep. At first his casts went at random along the favored bank. Don would coax, "Now just in front of that rock!"

After a while Gene caught on to the recognition of holding water, and plunked his nymph just upstream and again just downstream from the features that marked the few best spots along a bank. His percentage of hooked fish turned upward sharply, day by day, as the trip progressed.

But Gene's greatest progress began to occur when he learned to recognize water that was not likely to hold trout at all. Empty water is almost always featureless water. It might be a long pebbled riffle a foot or less deep, or a broad flat that is too thin to protect fish and has no depressions or trenches to provide even minimum shelter where a fish could dive in an emergency. The inside bend of a stream is often a gravelly flat that is too shallow to hold fish. Both current and depth tend toward the outside of a curve: most of the features and holding water will be found there, and most of the trout will be found there, too.

Water that is shallow and featureless is generally empty of trout because it does not offer sufficient protection from predators, or shelter from currents if the water is swift. But such water is sometimes rich in insect life, offering up concentrated hatches of mayflies, caddisflies, or stoneflies. When a hatch is happening on a stretch of empty water, that piece of water suddenly becomes the best feeding lie around. Trout know it and will move into it to feed, as I have said before, even at the risk of a tithe of one or more of them.

What you judge to be empty water should not be fished thoroughly unless there is some sign that fish hold or feed in it. But it should always be examined with a careful eye, and should often be probed with a few careful casts.

While I was drifting the Montana river with Gene and Don, we got whacked by a sudden thunderstorm. We dove for slickers, covered our gear with tarps, then drew our necks into our collars as far as we could and sat like turtles waiting for the rain to stop. It took two hours.

When the rain did stop, Gene and I stood up and began casting again. Through a two-hundred yard reach of river the water was shallow on both banks, inches deep at the edges, and only a foot or so deep about five feet out. We both cast idly to the banks, since there was no better water around, waiting for the boat to slide down to water that we considered worth fishing. But brown trout began climbing all over our Woolly Buggers. They erupted out of water so shallow it should not have held them.

Before we had gone the two hundred yards, we had each taken a couple of browns that approached a couple of pounds. They had moved up out of deep water, with the cooling rain, to forage on whatever might get active along the banks. They held in what I would normally have judged to be empty water, especially for fish of their size. But even then, they always struck the streamers from behind some slight feature: a football-sized rock, an overhanging tuft of bunchgrass, a cut where two shallow currents came together and disturbed the surface enough to disrupt overhead vision.

Water that is almost still will usually be empty of fish unless it is deep enough to be a prime lie for a large trout. But even in deep water, there must be sufficient current at the head of the still water to deliver food. Generally a pool that is surrounded above and below by fairly fast water will be a prime lie, while a long reach of deep but uniformly slow or still water will not be.

There is almost always some line of demarcation between empty water and water that promises to hold trout. It might be a surface seam where shallow and deeper currents meet, a deepening of the water that shows as a darkness on the surface, or a boulder or some other break to the current. Some shade, or some sweeping overhanging grass from the bank, will often be the only features on a long flat stretch of water, and they will indicate the only places trout might hold.

Where there is a demarcation line, or some sort of feature, it is always wise to fish it carefully. These are the sorts of things that denote lies, and lies are where you find fish.

5

Reading Riffles

Defined concisely, riffles are fast and shallow water, cobbled on the bottom and choppy on the surface. They are the richest parts of freestone streams, surpassed in productivity only by weed-filled reaches of meadow streams. Their voices are boisterous and eager and chatty; they speak of freedom and fun and good fishing.

STRUCTURE OF A RIFFLE

Riffles are the fast and shallow water that delivers the stream from run to run, or run to pool. They vary from a few inches to three or four feet deep. Their bottoms consist of rock, usually on the small side, from pebbles up to some the size of basketballs. Due to laws of hydraulics that are not well understood yet, at least by me, the size of the stones in a given riffle tends toward uniformity. But perfect uniformity is rarely attained; a riffle is usually broken by at least a few misfit boulders and rocks of a variety of sizes. These become holding lies for trout, though the trout fisherman cannot always see them through the broken surface of the riffle.

Riffles are spaced at fairly regular intervals along the course of a stream, generally at distances from five to seven stream widths apart. They are fixed and constant features; they do not move. Some of the stones that compose them, however, migrate individually downstream to the next riffle during high water and are replaced by stones bouncing down from the riffle above.

The largest stones tend to be deposited in the surface layers of a riffle's bottom structure. The deeper layers are composed successively of smaller stones, gravel and pebbles, and finally sand and silt as you go down into the substrate. This order of deposition causes myriad small spaces between stones, which become what entomologist Rick Hafele calls living rooms for aquatic insects. The larger spaces are on top, the smaller spaces distributed farther down. The great number of these places for insects to live are a lot of what makes a riffle so rich.

The roughness of a riffle's bottom is a direct result of the largest rocks being deposited in the upper layers of the streambed. Their migratory tendency means they are seldom firmly seated. That is why you sometimes feel like you're treading on a submerged field of rolling stones when you wade a riffle. You are.

The roughness of the cobbled bottom is reflected up to the riffle's surface. Part of the definition of a riffle is the choppiness on its surface. It helps you read water when you understand that what you see on the surface paints a reflected picture of what you can't see on the bottom.

THE NEEDS OF TROUT

Some riffles hold trout, some don't. Those that do hold trout meet the needs of the fish consistently and coax them to establish and stay on territories. Riffles that don't hold trout fail to meet one or another of the basic needs and are not constantly good places for the fish to be. But they might hold trout at specific times. For example, a brisk riffle that lacks obstructions to the current behind which fish can rest, might hold fish temporarily during a heavy hatch of insects.

Shelter from Currents

The need for shelter from currents is the key need of trout in a riffle. The rest of a trout's needs are met with abundance. Recall that the ultimate quality of a trout's territory is based not on the amount of feed it provides, but on the amount of shelter it gives from the current and the protection it gives from predators.

Most riffles have lots of small niches offering shelter to small fish. They are excellent rearing areas for fry and fingerlings. But it takes some modest-sized stones in the current to hold fish of the size we don't mind catching, say from nine inches to a foot or more long. In most riffles there are plenty of scattered rocks, small boulders, and other features that break the current along the bottom. In most streams, riffles hold the most trout, and are the first place to fish if you are after fast action.

You will find the kind of fish you would rather catch, from a foot to sixteen inches long, only around larger breaks in the riffle's current. Every productive riffle has a few of these, and every one will hold a trout, its size depending on the size of the territory the obstruction forms.

Fish much bigger than sixteen inches are rare in riffles, simply because lies of the size they need are not often found in shallow water.

Protection from Predators

The choppy surface of a riffle is a broken window to vision from above. Protection from predators is excellent. Most birds and beasts hunt their fish in slow or still water. Trout in riffles seem to enjoy a great sense of security. They are not as nervous as they are in most other types of water.

The broken surface of a riffle works against most predators, but it works for you and me. We can wade closer to trout without alarming them. We can fish from in close, with short casts and lots of control over the line and fly. This is important; the closer you can work to a fish in rough water the more chance you have of presenting your fly correctly and detecting a take when it happens.

Trout Foods in Riffles

Riffles meet the trout's need for food graciously. Two things make it so. First, there are all those little living rooms for insects. Second, photosynthetic plant growth on riffle rocks, caused by sunlight striking down through the shallow water, gives the same insects lots of fine pastures to browse. Riffles are constant conveyors of nymphs and larvae that get dislodged by the current. A trout waiting on its station with its window on a slice of the riffle's current sees them passing and makes its living by dashing out to intercept as many as it possibly can.

Aquatic insects are the primary source of food for trout in riffles, though terrestrial insects are sometimes surprised to find themselves awash in the water and taken into the drift that constantly moves through. Most of the time, riffle trout feed on a mixture of this and that, with various stages of a variety of insect species being delivered down the currents. The aquatic insects of riffles consist primarily of mayflies, caddisflies, and stoneflies. These are the bits of food that riffle trout eat most often.

Mayflies, as outlined in the chapter on trout foods, have a three-stage life cycle: from nymph to dun to spinner. Mayfly nymphs that live in riffles are mostly among the flat clinger and robust crawler varieties. These are able to cling tenaciously to stones in fast currents. They live down in the smaller niches of the substrate in their youth, coming out into the current on the tops of rocks only to feed. But as they mature, which is usually in spring and early summer, they move up into larger niches, they get restless, and they get taken by trout much more often.

Many mayfly species migrate before emergence, crossing the bottom in the nymphal stage in order to emerge as duns in calmer water near shore. During these migrations they march in their thousands right through the territories of hungry trout. This behavior is the basis for much of the best nymph fishing we enjoy in riffles.

A lot of other mayfly species emerge out in midriffle. The nymph fastens itself to bottom stones with its tarsal claws, the chitinous skin along its back splits open, and the dun emerges right there. It is then tossed at the whim of the current on its wild ride to the surface. When a lot of these come off it is an obvious cause for excitement among trout. It appears to be a time for dry-

Clinger mayfly nymphs from a riffle.

fly fishing, because what the angler sees, with his distant view, is a flock of duns riding the chop. But a wet fly fished under the surface mimics the arising dun and will often take more fish than a dry.

Once the duns reach the surface they must ride it out until their wings dry and they can fly. Because the surface is rough, many are drowned and are taken underwater and into the swirling drift. Again, it seems like dry-fly time, but wets are often better.

Duns that survive fly to streamside vegetation, where they molt into spinners before returning to mate and lay their eggs. Most egg laying takes place over runs and flats, not riffles, though spent mayfly spinners drown and are delivered downstream to riffles as a major component of the drift.

Riffle-dwelling caddisfly larvae are primarily free-living; they don't build cases. They are wormlike, cannot swim, and are frequently dislodged by the current for the convenience of forag-

ing trout. Their presence in good numbers is an indication that
nymphing the bottom will be an excellent way to fool fish.

When their full growth is achieved, caddis larvae seal themselves into submerged cocoons, and the pupal transformation
into the adult form takes place there. When it is complete they
cut out of the cocoons and make their way to the surface.

Caddis pupae are among the most exciting and most invisible
insects in riffles. Though some can swim, for the most part they
are at the whim of the current until they reach the surface. But a
riffle is shallow; it's a brief transition and trout know it. They
rush caddis pupae eagerly, often making the successful intercep-
tion just beneath the surface so that their momentum rockets
them into the air above the riffle. It is odd behavior, and almost
always indicates trout feeding on the pupal stage of the caddis,
not the adult.

It is also confusing behavior because what we see, from our
viewpoint above the water, are not pupal caddis but escaping
adults that have survived the trip to the top and shot off into the
air. Trout feed on the pupae, but their swirls and splashes are at
the surface and they appear to be feeding on adults. I used to try
every dry fly I owned in these instances, while the trout fed
greedily just under the surface and ignored them all. I've learned
that switching to a subsurface nymph or wet fly approximately
the size and color of the adult will usually turn the trick and take
at least a few of the trout.

Even when caddis are not emerging, a lot of caddis adults are
still out and about, busy bouncing above riffles, laying eggs, and
getting eaten by trout. Fish get used to seeing the caddis shape
and seem quite eager to spear upward out of their shallow holds
to take it. The most successful dry flies that I have used for riffle
fishing are based on the natural shape of the caddisfly adult.

Stoneflies, though numerous in riffles, are a hidden insect. The
nymphs live in their niches among the stones. When ready to
emerge, they crawl in their migrations toward shore. Trout seldom feed selectively on them, but they do eat a lot of them,
usually as individual items picked up along the buffet line that is
the riffle's current. They add to the various mayfly nymphs and
caddisfly larvae and other unhappy creatures that make up the
drift on which riffle trout feed most of the time. They increase

the reasons that bumping a weighted nymph along the bottom is an effective tactic in a riffle.

Because stoneflies crawl out to emerge, usually at night, their actual hatches are seldom events that interest any but sleepless anglers. But many stonefly adults deposit their eggs over afternoon and evening riffles. They are an important source of food. They don't often cause trout in riffles to feed selectively, but they do cause trout to turn their attention toward the surface so you can entice them up to a dry fly.

Mayflies, caddisflies, and stoneflies make up the bulk of the diet for riffle trout. Other creatures find themselves inserted into the menu from time to time. These include cranefly and midge larvae, various terrestrials such as beetles and ants, and a modest amount of oligochaetes – true worms. But most often these are taken as swirling snacks rather than main meals.

Temperature and Oxygen Levels

Riffles are rich in oxygen, second only to frothed rapids and cascades. As we have seen, temperature and oxygen are interrelated needs. When rivers suffer summer low flows and trout begin to get distressed, the fish move to the most aerated water. If there are no springheads or feeder streams, they will often hang in riffles, or in the nearest suitable holding water below them, to take advantage of the freshness of the stream.

If conditions are extreme and you find no trout holding in riffles, the next logical choice is to fish pocket water, or to explore until you discover cool springs or shaded headwaters. Sometimes trout will move up into tiny creeks, and you will find them there in sizes and numbers all out of proportion to what the creek could be expected to provide.

Whenever you hook a fish that is already stressed by the conditions of the stream, you risk its life. Land it quickly and release it gently. If conditions are marginal for trout survival you should not fish at all.

HOLDING LIES IN RIFFLES

Holding riffles, as opposed to feeding riffles or barren riffles, have at least a few breaks in the current where trout can set up stations and defend territories. One of the major dimensions of any territory is its depth, and riffles are always limited in that dimension. The food-producing area of any territory is its bottom, and secondarily its surface. A territory set up in shallow water is not going to be as large as a territory in deeper water.

Since the size of a fish is limited by the size of its territory, even a riffle that has good holding lies throughout its length usually holds trout somewhat smaller than the largest that can be caught from the given stream. But the aquatic life of a riffle, combined with the high number of compact niches it offers to trout, makes it a good place to start a day on any stream. If you are not a bounty hunter only after trophies, it might be a good place to spend the day.

You can catch lots of trout in riffles.

Empty Water

Pinpointing potential holding lies in a riffle, and finding its fish, is relatively easy. The first thing to do is to eliminate the empty water; on paper, this means the water that is only a few inches deep, too thin to protect trout. It also means the dead water off to the sides of the riffle, where there is no current to deliver food. You can eliminate a whole riffle if it is shallow and unfeatured, or if it flows too swiftly and without breaks so trout could not hold there.

On the stream, empty water should be dismissed with a little more caution. Fly-fishing literature is full of scoldings for those of us who assume a certain kind of water would never hold a trout. Scan the skinny water, especially if it is bumpy and hard to see into, to see if it might not hide feeding trout or have hidden features that would shelter trout. Look for signs of a hatch; lots of insect types migrate right to the shore before emerging. Trout sometimes follow and feed on them in water where they would not otherwise be found.

Once you have eliminated the empty water, it is time to examine the potential holding water to see just where trout are most likely to be found in it. There are several obvious places to search, with your eyes and your flies. You are looking for high-

Fishing the corner of a riffle.

percentage water, and it is the way the water meets the needs of the trout that propels it into that category.

Since most of a riffle offers protection from predators and lots of food, shelter from currents is the obvious thing to look for when you look for holding lies in fast and shallow water. Any part of the riffle that satisfies all three needs of the trout will be a prime lie and is likely to be the spot where you find the largest trout.

Corner of a Riffle

The head of a riffle is the first obvious place to look for holding lies, and it is the most likely place in the whole stream to find a few trout. Watch fishing guides work, especially on a boating river; you will see them ease their boats down through pools and runs and rapids, encouraging their clients to cast. But they will always pull over, beach the boat, and fish them carefully at the edges of riffles.

It is not the top end of the riffle itself that should draw your attention: it is the two slight eddies formed at each corner. These are the wedges of water squeezed in between the rough riffle on the outside and the still water that is against the shore on the inside. They are slight triangles, little bigger than a yachtsman's flag on tiny riffles, still not much wider than the length of a short cast on larger riffles.

The best way to describe this water is to tell you that it is always where you will see somebody wade right in to begin fishing the part of the riffle out beyond it, where the water looks a lot more fishy but holds a lot fewer fish.

The corner of a riffle is usually just a foot or two deep. It is slightly rough on top, but not as choppy as the riffle outside of it, and not as smooth as the backed-up water to the inside. It is a transitional line of water, down along the edge of the riffle, that varies from a foot wide to about fifteen feet wide. It might extend for just a few feet, it might follow the riffle on down for fifty feet or so.

It is amazing the number of fish you can draw up, even from the tiniest corner. You should absolutely never wade into a riffle until you have popped a few casts to the water that looks like it shouldn't hold any fish.

Jim Schollmeyer, the well-known fishing photographer, and I worked a long riffle on the Bighorn River in the fall of eighty-seven. I started in about thirty feet below the head of the riffle, feeling the pressure of needing to provide Jim a fish to photograph, and slowly worked my way up toward the corner. Jim stood on the bank behind me, resting his camera on a tripod, waiting for me to hook a fish. I didn't do it soon. I fished right up into the corner without a rise, felt embarrassed, but didn't know what to do besides give up.

From his higher vantage point, Jim spotted a fish rising. He homed me in on it. "Farther up!" he said.

I thought I had already fished the corner out to its end, but I moved up and took a couple more casts to where there was almost no water left. Nothing rose to the fly and I looked up at Jim to get more directions. "Farther up!" he ordered again. "Farther up!"

I made a cast to where the corner was the size of an arrowhead point. A trout took with a subtle swirl, felt the hook, and pounced out into the current. It used the force of the river to drive it, and I was forced to splash after it. Jim snapped pictures when I finally led it into quiet water two hundred feet down the riffle. It was a rainbow, about three pounds, but it fought above its weight.

We talked idly while we walked through bankside grasses back to the head of the riffle, Jim carrying his camera and tripod slung over his shoulder, me carrying my fly rod slung over mine. I was going to go on beyond the corner and up to the boat. It was time to float down and join our friends for lunch. But Jim said, "Take another cast up there," and pointed at the corner.

I said, "What for?"

"Just in case," Jim answered.

I did and another fish took with the same subtle swirl, took off with the same river-propelled flight. We wound up landing it in the same spot, Jim took the same pictures all over again, and I released the trout. This one weighed closer to four pounds.

These were uncommonly large trout to be holding in a riffle, but the Bighorn is an uncommon river. Never neglect the corner of a riffle on any river.

Tail of Riffle

A lot of life is produced in the length of a riffle. A lot of it is dislodged daily. The lower down the riffle, the more chance that bits of life will be adrift on the current.

If the riffle has obstructions throughout its length, trout will hold wherever they can, according to the shelter provided from the current. But if the riffle has few places where trout can hold, it will be used as a feeding riffle, or not be used at all.

If a featureless riffle is less than boisterous, trout will move up into it to feed whenever insects are active. If the current is fast, though, trout would tire in it quickly. Instead of moving into it, they hold where the riffle breaks, at its lowest end, and wait for the current to deliver drift farther down. This is transitional water, sometimes a shallow sort of tailout where the water shelves up a bit, sometimes merging into whatever kind of water comes next: a run or a pool.

If water nearby offers shelter from currents and protection from predators, and if there is a hatch or some other insect activity going on in the length of a riffle where trout do not hold, then they will often move up into the lower end of the feeding riffle, remaining there only so long as there is enough food available to keep them ahead in the energy equation. When the food supply dwindles they drop down to other kinds of water.

Obstructions in Riffles

It becomes slowly obvious that the key to holding water in riffles is any obstruction that slows the current. It is also evident that, because a riffle tends to accumulate evenly sized rocks and to conceal them beneath a uniformly choppy surface, these obstructions don't always expose themselves readily to the angler's eye.

The most common obstruction that forms a holding lie in a riffle is a small gathering of rocks, slightly larger than the stones on the riffle bed around them, that deflects the current in several directions, causing turbulence, amidst which there is usually a place where the water is slower. This becomes a trout's station, and the water around it the trout's territory.

These kinds of stations, ranging from small ones that hold tiny trout up to larger ones that sometimes show on the surface and usually hold larger trout, are scattered throughout the length of most riffles. They are the lies that Ray Bergman referred to in his famous 1938 *Trout,* when he said about riffles, "I wager that nine-tenths of the anglers skip them, considering them unworthy of notice. Some of them are – no doubt about it. But others have from one to ten *pocket holes* that contain fish."

Many prime lies in a riffle are marked on its surface. The most obvious among these are any boulders that either break the surface or reach toward it far enough to cause a boil on top. Any rock large enough to disrupt the surface is large enough to shelter a trout from the current.

Water pillows in front of a rock, and this creates a soft spot in the current just as effectively as the eddied water behind the rock. Because the pillow of slow water gives a trout an up-current view that is unobstructed by the rock, it is often a more efficient place for a trout to lie on station and survey its territory for bits of drift.

Though the literature is full of instructions to fish thoroughly in the broken water downstream from midstream rocks, I have taken a lot more trout from the water immediately upstream from them. Don't neglect the water below, but always be sure that if a fish is holding upstream from a rock, or any other obstruction in the current, it gets at least a fair look at your fly.

Ledges, Trenches, and Shelves

Ledges and trenches break the current and form lies for trout. They are generally structures of base-rock bottoms and are not common in riffles because riffles have cobbled bottoms. But

Photographer Jim Schollmeyer releasing a typical trout taken from the visible holding lies of a shallow riffle.

there are streams where riffles work their way to bedrock in a few places, and the water erodes shelves into shale and leaves undercuts that trout can creep under. A base-rock ledge or trench in the middle of a riffle will show as a smooth slick in the choppy surface.

A trench in a riffle forms a prime lie. It offers a shield against the current. Its depth provides overhead protection from predators. The riffle itself, with its richness of insect life, provides feed. If a riffle is to hold a trout that pushes beyond the pound mark, this is the kind of lie that will hold it.

There are lots of such lies on the Firehole River, in the Nez Perce Flats mileage of the river. This is a riffled section alternating with flats, most of it a foot or two deep. There is a lot of volcanic bedrock beneath the riffles, and the bedrock is pocked with depressions that are a foot or two deeper than the rest of the water. Most of these record themselves on the surface as slight slicks.

Fishing these Firehole riffles is easy once you catch on to wading downstream, dropping a dry ahead of you onto the water above the slicks. It also works well to cast a wet or small nymph above and beyond the lies, letting it sweep slowly down and across them on the current. Sometimes you will see a swirl as a fish takes in a patch of smooth water; other times you will feel your line tighten slowly, then feel a sullen pull, before you raise the rod to pull the hook into a trout that intercepted your fly as it crossed above its holding lie.

There are areas in riffles where the gravel suddenly shelves off. The drop is never as abrupt as it is in bedrock, but the sides slope steeply into deeper water. Probably the best way to describe one of these is to remind you of the time you were wading shallow, without a care, then took one more step and suddenly felt the gravel go out from under you. You backpedaled furiously; what you kept yourself from falling into was a fine trout lie at the foot of a sloping gravel shelf.

These gravel shelves usually run at angles across the current, though some run parallel to it. They are among the finest trout lies in riffles and hold some of the largest trout found in them. The shelf breaks the current, the depth of the water gives some protection from predation. The swirl of the current in the pocket causes food to gather and eddy, which makes it easy for trout to get it.

Shelves usually show up on the water as lines where the waves are suddenly and obviously different than they are throughout the rest of the riffle. The difference is usually easy to see, and you will have no trouble picking them out. Sometimes small shelves cause no more than a minor depression in the bottom. These are more difficult to spot, showing up only as areas where the waves are either a bit higher or a bit lower than the waves around them, or as patches of slightly darker water on the surface of the riffle.

Even small depressions hold trout, and you should fish them carefully.

Current Seams

Current seams are the sewing together of two currents either of different direction, or of different speeds. Wherever this happens, feed delivered by both currents gathers in one spot and trout find it a fine feeding lie. If the currents conflict enough to cause turbulence, and therefore some pockets of subdued flow, trout will establish holding lies beneath a seam.

Recognizing seams becomes such a sixth sense that an experienced fisherman will angle his casts along one without even noticing he has done it. Yet when he stands in the riffle and tries to point out what demarks the line, he can't do it. The difference is usually in the chop on the surface. Wherever you see a line of water with waves slightly sharper, taller or shorter, or just more agitated than those alongside it, consider it a likely place to hold trout. Fish the entire seam, placing your casts so the fly covers the center line and both sides of the seam.

The seam along the edge of a riffle is the easiest seam to see, and it is always a likely lie. This is especially true where the water at the side is shallow and slow, the water of the riffle two or three feet deep and much faster. The seam is clearly defined, with the smooth water to the side abutted against water out in the riffle that is choppy, and also darker due to the sudden acquiring of some depth. Such edges should always be carefully fished; trout often hang along their entire lengths.

Whitefish Water

Whitefish prefer moderate-to-fast riffles that are relatively featureless. Since whitefish and trout seldom hold together in the
same water, learning to spot their kind of water is one way of
limiting your fishing in what I have called empty water, assuming you would rather catch trout than whitefish. Wherever you
start catching bunches of whitefish, jog off and fish somewhere
else, unless you're like me and you don't care enough about what
kind of fish you catch.

It is best not to carelessly dismiss a particular piece of stream
as whitefish water. While on a trip recently with some rigid
antiwhitefish fishermen, I saw a flock of fish rising with the tiny
blips characteristic of what my companions derisively called
"rubbernoses," actually an apt description. We had not had many
chances to fish over rising fish on the trip, and I had a craving for
that kind of fishing. I didn't care what kind of fish they were.

I hopped over the side of the boat, bounced along holding the
gunwhale for a few feet while my feet explored for the bottom,
then let the boat go and said breathlessly, "I'll catch up with you
around the next corner." I'd thought the water was shallow. They
wouldn't have pulled over to let me off anyway.

I looked closely for a few seconds at the water where the fish
rose. It was a riffle about three feet deep. A few #16 Blue-Winged
Olive duns rode its surface. I hastily added two feet of two-
pound-test tippet, then tied on a small olive-bodied dun-hackled
wet fly. I dressed the fly with floatant, cast it out, and fished it
dry. A fish took without hesitation, with the same blip it had
been making for the tiny naturals. It reacted violently to the
hook. It fought eagerly and well. It was a rainbow trout.

I caught only three or four more, between twelve and fourteen
inches long, before I had to reel up and huff off in a panic to catch
up with the boat. I didn't expect my partners to wait long for a
whitefish fisherman. When I caught up with them at the next
corner and told them what the fish were, they didn't believe me.

"That was whitefish water," one of them said, "and those were
whitefish rises. Now get in the boat and let's go fish for some
trout."

STRATEGIES FOR FISHING RIFFLES

Selectivity is not usually an aspect of trout behavior in riffles. They feed at random, from the drift, most of the time. Their posture on their stations is one of readiness to move out and intercept bits of food. Their focus will be on whatever level of water has been providing them the most grub. Most of the time this is the bottom, but a riffle is shallow, and they are often attuned to drift at mid-depths or on the top.

Though most people turn instantly to dry flies when fishing riffles, it is best to think in terms of the three levels at which trout feed: the bottom, mid-depths, and top. Even though the water is shallow, fish with their attention on one of the levels will sometimes ignore flies presented at one of the other levels.

Tackle for Fishing Riffles

Tackle for fishing the three levels of a riffle is all the same, unless you happen to command a caddy and can shout him up with another rod at the slightest change in the situation.

Most of my riffle fishing is done with an eight-foot rod that casts a five-weight double-taper dry line. This reflects my own prejudice. Most people prefer rods eight and a half to nine feet long, and I agree with them (though I'll stick with the rod I use because I've used it for a long time; we don't argue like we used to, and sometimes I win now).

The double-taper dry line is my preference for most fishing, and I don't switch unless I have to. I find no need to switch in order to fish the three levels of a riffle. The dry line allows me more control over the drift of a weighted nymph, and gives me a report when a trout intercepts the imitation down there where I can't see it happen. It fishes wet flies just under the surface, which is where I want them, and dry flies on top of the surface, which is also where I want them. The double-taper is easier to mend and tend than is a weight-forward taper. It casts almost as far, and I seldom cast very far anyway.

The five-weight line seems just right for all but high winds and heavy nymphs. If I fished a lot when the wind was blowing, or cast a lot with large leaded flies, I would use a rod balanced to a six- or seven-weight line. At times I do anyway, when I'm on a big river, but most of the time I like the lighter line, and my caddy is never behind me when I holler for something heavier.

A leader about the length of the rod is all you really need in a riffle. I buy or tie nine-foot knotted leaders with tips one size stouter than I intend to use. On the stream I add a two-foot tippet of the strength I want, and have a leader a couple of feet longer than I need. For fishing wets or drys, the point is usually three-pound-test, for nymphs it is four- to six-pound-test. Whatever leader you use, it should gracefully turn over the flies you cast with it.

Fishing the Bottom

The best approach for fishing the bottom of a riffle is with the upstream nymph technique. Start at the lower end of the riffle and work your way slowly toward the top. If the water is a couple of feet deep or more and looks like it might have hidden lies throughout its length, set up a pattern and fish all of the water.

Start by casting almost straight upstream, then make each successive cast a couple of feet farther out into the riffle. Continue until you've worked all of the water you can from the initial position without casting more than thirty-five to forty feet. Keep the casts shorter if the water and your self-discipline allow it. Then wade upstream a few feet and repeat the pattern.

If the riffle has the potential for holding trout anywhere, it is best to fish prime lies only as you come to them. Then fish them thoroughly, working the fly into the water above and below boulders, deep into trenches, along ledges, and down on the bottom beneath any seams where two currents meet. Read the water for the most likely holding lies; present your flies diligently where fish are most likely to hold.

When you are fishing the bottom, your fly selection should be related to the natural insects that dwell there. For the most part, as already pointed out, these are mayfly nymphs, stonefly nymphs, and free-living caddisfly larvae. They run the hook size scale from tiny twenties up to number four. On the average,

Fly selection for fishing the top, mid-depths, and bottom of a riffle.

though, they run in the midrange of hook sizes, from number twelve through number eight, and it is the average that trout see and eat most of the time.

The colors of the most common naturals run to dark grays, olives, and browns. They blend with bottom stones.

A refined fishing vest, bulging with fly boxes, will house an incredible collection of imitative nymphs. But a few general patterns, searching nymphs, are usually most effective in riffles. Don't do as I did when I began my fly-fishing career; I matched all the rarities and oddities I found, and wound up with a collection—a tangle—of dressings that imitated creatures I had seen only once, and most trout had not seen at all.

To cover the size and color spectrum of most naturals, one would need to carry only a few Gray Nymphs, Gold-Ribbed Hare's Ears, and olive-bodied Zug Bugs in sizes eight through

twelve. They should be slightly weighted, and you should carry
BB split shot or twist-on lead to get them down to the bottom
when their internal weight is not enough. The speed and depth of
the water will dictate the amount of weight needed.

A bright strike indicator on the leader will help you spot the
hesitation that marks the take of a nymph. The indicator should
be above the fly about twice the depth of the water. This allows
the fly a natural drift while keeping the indicator on the surface
where you can see it. The indicator can be a bit of red yarn tied to
the leader, a large and bushy dry fly, or any of the commercial
indicators available at fly shops. I use a #10 flame-colored Corky,
a tiny round lure used by steelheaders here on the West Coast. It
floats and it is easy to see, but it is not big enough or buoyant
enough to boss the drift of the fly.

Few nymphs that live in riffles swim well. When they are
dislodged from their hold on the bottom they tumble along with
the current until they are able to retrieve their footing. You want
your fly to perform approximately the same maneuvers, tumbling along in what is commonly called a *dead drift presentation*.
In order to achieve that you're almost forced to fish upstream.

Upstream nymph presentation calls for wading into a position
close to the water you want to fish. If you cast much more than
forty feet you will seldom either detect a take or react to it in
time to set the hook. It is best to fish twenty to thirty feet out;
sometimes trout will take almost under your rod tip. You can fish
that close to them in riffles.

The first casts should be made at a slight angle out from
straight upstream. The fly should sink quickly to the bottom.
Hold the rod tip high enough to keep as much line off the water
as possible, but not so high that you have no reach left with
which to rear back and set the hook. Then follow the indicator
down with the rod, drawing in slack as the fly tumbles toward
you, dropping the rod tip and feeding out slack as the fly passes
you and drifts downstream. When it has reached the end of the
drift, let the current lift it up from the bottom. Strikes will often
occur at this point, though you will miss a lot of them because in
setting the hook you draw it away from the fish instead of into its
jaw.

The indicator should ride on or just an inch or two under the surface. This is difficult fishing at first. It takes some practice to get the feel for what is a take and what is not. The best rule is this: If the indicator hesitates at all, set the hook. Sometimes it will be a fish, sometimes not. But if you don't set the hook, you will never know.

At times the indicator will take a sudden bounce forward that spells an obvious strike. Most often, takes are more subtle. The fish merely noses over from its station, intercepts the fly, mouths it, doesn't like the taste, and rejects it. Meanwhile, the indicator has hesitated. It is almost imperceptible. The surprising thing in this kind of fishing is the number of trout you will hook once you get the hang of it. And you will rarely be able to tell just what it was that triggered your strike. When striking becomes a sixth sense, you have upstream nymph fishing down.

Fishing Mid-depths in Riffles

Fishing mid-depths can be done with the same nymphs used for fishing the bottom without any weight added to the leader, which makes them more versatile. But the insects trout find adrift at mid-depths are more often either emerging stages with their legs and antennae trailing in the currents, or drowned terrestrials and winged aquatic adults. These have more moving parts than nymphs, and are perfectly imitated by either traditional wet flies or simple soft-hackled wets.

The patterns that work best for me in riffles are standard wets such as the Light and Dark Cahills, and soft-hackles such as the Partridge and Green, Partridge and Yellow, and March Brown Spider. Typical sizes are just a bit smaller than the nymphs used to fish the bottom: sizes ten, twelve, and fourteen.

To fish mid-depths with a wet fly, step in at the head of the riffle, cast slightly downstream from straight across, and allow the fly to swing around slowly with the current. When the fly starts to swing too fast, slow it by mending the line, lifting up the downstream curve of the line and looping it over back upstream. What you should strive to achieve is a drift in which the line leads the fly like a poodle on a leash. This brings it down broadside to the current, giving fish the best look at it. But it should not travel faster than a natural insect might swim.

Set up a pattern, casting short at first, then work each cast farther out until you are fishing forty-five feet of line. This is a comfortable distance at which you can control the drift and mend the line. When your casts are extended to the full distance, begin taking a couple of steps downstream between casts, and you will present your fly to any hidden lies along the length of the riffle. Fish the entire riffle if it is deep enough and slow enough that fish might hold anywhere along it.

When you come to any prime lie, slow down and fish your casts out more carefully. Try to fish in closer, and tend the drift of the fly so that it probes in and around the lie. Mend the line so that the fly hangs in the water where you would expect a trout to lie.

If the riffle is shallow and fast, appearing to be either empty water or bordering on it, stalk only the prime lies. Fish them from upstream and off to the side. You will often take fish from surprising places this way. They will hold behind rocks of soft-ball size in just inches of water at times. But you are not likely to catch large trout from this type of water. They hold in prime lies where the water is at least a couple of feet deep.

Fishing the Surface of a Riffle

Fishing dry is the easiest, and often the most productive, way to explore a riffle. Dry-fly fishing in fast water is far easier than fishing upstream nymphs, and a little easier than fishing wet flies if you fish them beyond the chuck-and-chance-it level.

Trout in riffles are seldom selective unless there is a whopping hatch in progress. Still, a fly pattern that is chosen for its resemblance to a lot of the insects that trout eat in riffles will catch a lot more fish for you than a fly resembling nothing riffle trout have ever seen.

Because adult caddis are so active, out and bouncing about so much during the daylight hours, the best flies with which to explore the tops of riffles are impressionistic caddis patterns. The best dressings I have found are the light-colored Elk Hair Caddis and the darker Deer Hair Caddis, usually in sizes twelve and fourteen.

These two dressings resemble the most common types of riffle

Fishing a dry fly upstream in a riffle.

caddisflies. They float well. The Elk Hair is very visible, even in failing light. But there are times when the brighter fly fails to draw up fish. Whenever this happens switch to the drab Deer Hair Caddis; fish seem willing to come up for it if they are willing to come up for anything at all. But riffle trout won't often ignore you if you show up to fish them with Royal Wulffs, Humpies, or any other favorite dry fly patterns you possess. Fish with the flies in which you have the most confidence, because riffle trout are seldom selective.

When fishing dry it is best to start at the foot of the riffle, as you did with the deep nymph, and work your way upstream. Each cast should be made at an angle that is at least a little off straight upstream, in order to keep the line from sailing over the fish before the fly lights above it. Each successive cast should work a bit farther out, the drift covering a slice of water a foot or two from the first, until the water above you is covered in a disciplined fashion. Then wade ten to fifteen feet upstream and cover another section of the riffle. Don't stop until you have reached the very corner of the corner.

If the water is not deep enough to hold trout throughout the riffle, work your dry-fly casts over just the prime holding lies. Be sure to cover the water at the edges of the current, along any seams, and above and below any obstructions.

If you fail to bring fish up from what look like prime lies, chances are the riffle does not hold trout at all, or holds them only when insects are active. If the tactics for fishing the three levels fail to produce for you in a given riffle, it is time to give up on the riffle and drop down to fish the run below.

6

Finding Fish in Runs

Runs are where riffles go when all the excitement is over. In most trout stream situations runs are relatively fast-flowing water between three and six feet deep, with fairly even depth and current speed from the head down to the tail.

STRUCTURE OF A RUN

Runs vary from about a foot and a half deep in the smallest creeks up to eight or ten feet deep in the largest trout rivers. They tend to be deepest, in cross section, where the flow is strongest, usually in the center of the run if the run is straight. If a run is located on a curve in the river, it tends to deepen toward the outside and shallow up toward the inside. Some runs, especially those that are so gentle they approach being flats, carry almost the same depth from side to side.

Many runs gradually deepen as they move from the head to the tail. A common case would be a run that is three to four feet deep at the head and five to six feet deep at the tailout. But there are

no abrupt drops or the water would suddenly slow down and it would be a pool instead of a run.

The head of a run usually receives a riffle. The water is chopped at the upper end and gradually calms as it moves toward the lower end. Runs have a tendency to be narrower at the head, spreading out a bit as they move down and deepen. The lower end of the run sometimes spills straight into whatever kind of water comes next, usually another riffle or a deep pool. But most of the time there is a lifting tailout over a buildup of cobble and stones before the water drops over and down.

The gradient of a run is not as steep as the gradient of a riffle.

Runs are not so swift, though most have strong flows. Their surfaces are smoother than riffles, lacking the choppiness that reflects shallow water flowing swiftly over a cobbled bottom.

The slightly slower current of a run allows finer sediment to drop out of the water and settle to the bottom. As a result, the predominant bottom material tends more to small rocks, pebbles, and coarse sand, rather than the uniform cobble of riffles. It is more compact and does not have nearly the number of spaces between rocks that are found in riffles. Overlaid on the finer bottom, in freestone stream runs, is a deposition of rocks and boulders much larger than those found in riffles.

Anybody who has stumbled over the uneven stones of a pushy run can tell you about its bottom. You can nearly jog through many riffles, but you creep through runs, feeling your way ahead with a staff like a blind man probing for surprises with his cane.

Meadow-stream runs have most of the structural characteristics of typical freestone runs. Their depths tend toward three to six feet, fairly even from side to side and end to end. They shallow toward the inside of a curve and deepen toward the outside. But they lack the bouldery bottoms. There might be an occasional large rock that the stream has eroded its way around; for the most part the bottom consists of pebbles, gravel, and in some cases sediment.

The smooth bottom of a meadow-stream run is reflected up to a glassy surface. The surface of a freestone run is calm where the bottom is fine, but rougher where it flows over rock and boulders. Boils and slicks quarrel on the surface where large obstructions break the current on the bottom. If the run is fast and has boulders breaking its surface, it will have some white water and will sing a loud song.

NEEDS OF TROUT

The structure of a run differs from that of a riffle, and it meets the needs of trout in different ways. Runs often hold the trout that move in and out of feeding riffles. Because runs offer larger territories, they usually receive the trout that outgrow riffles and move toward bigger water. If your goal is to catch larger trout, one way to achieve it is to spend more time fishing runs, less time fishing shallow riffles.

Shelter from Currents

The larger rocks found on the bottom of a run have obvious implications when we start to analyze how they meet the need for shelter from currents. But there is another factor to crank in first: the gradient of a run is not as steep, the current is not so rushing, and the need for shelter from it, though still a major factor, is not quite so critical as it is in a swift riffle.

The boulders along the bottom of a run interrupt the flow,

creating dozens of the kinds of lies that are only occasional in riffles. They also cause turbulence, which sounds bad at first. Turbulence creates holding lies even where bottom stones are not individually large enough to form them. The word "turbulence" brings up violent connotations. But take a deep breath, clasp your nose, go down below, and pretend you're a trout. Lie near the bottom of a run. Here comes the water right at you, with all its force. Hold your breath, brace yourself, and get ready to wag your tail with all your might. It looks like you're going to have to swim a sprint just to stay where you are.

But a bunch of medium-sized stones, just upstream from your lie, bounce the current back and forth between them. The result is a bunch of swirls and eddies that would only be visible if somebody above you poured dye into the water. But what you *feel*, as a trout hugging the bottom, already taking advantage of the rules of friction that slow the water in a thin layer there, are small soft spots of gentle water where the currents cancel each other. You can hold without much effort at all.

You've been a good trout. Come on up now.

The general trend of turbulence, according to hydrologists, is upward, away from the bottom that causes it. Because of both friction and turbulence, the layer of slow water along the bottom of a run is substantial, much more than that offered in a riffle. Shelter from strong currents, therefore, is offered in a lot more places, and trout find a lot more water where they can hold in comfort in a run.

The obvious exception to this is the run without much on its bottom to break the current. Even if the flow is relatively easy, a trout will not fight it constantly. If there are no obstructions, there will be very few trout. Read the water; if it is featureless, it will usually be troutless.

Protection from Predators

Protection from predators is offered primarily by the greater depth of the run. The surface of a run is, if not a broken window like the surface of a riffle, at least a distorted window, like an old and dirty pane of glass. Overhead predators cannot see trout through it clearly unless the trout are feeding high in the water, holding up near the surface. When trout are on their stations, down near the bottom, distortion combines with the dimness of three to six feet of depth to make them nearly impossible to detect.

Not many aerial predators could puncture enough water to take a fish at the depths that they commonly hold in runs anyway. But runs are happy hunting grounds for diving birds like mergansers, and also for the sleek whiskered death that is the working end of an otter. Trout are aware of it.

Trout are alert in proportion to the geography of a run. If it is fast and broken they will feel relatively secure. If it is mild and smooth they will have their senses honed for danger. You must make an assessment of the kind of water they are in and approach each according to its kind. If you always err on the side of quiet and caution, you will seldom frighten your fish. You might

All the boulders, visible and invisible, form potential prime lies in a run.

even seen an otter. If you jog right up in a shower of spray you can't expect to catch fish no matter where they hold.

Trout Foods in Runs

A run, with its compact bottom, does not have an excess of the tiny spaces between rocks that form living rooms for insects. Penetration of sunlight determines the amount of weed and algal growth, which is the basis for insect populations. Photosynthetic growth on bottom rocks is substantial in runs two to four feet deep, especially if the water is clear as glass. But deeper runs, and those that are slightly opaque from water that is not perfectly clean, cut off sunlight and lack lots of growth.

Runs are not insect-poor. Their aquatic insect populations rest somewhere between the low populations of pools and the densities found in riffles. The insect groups tend to be the same as those found in riffles: mayfly nymphs, stonefly nymphs, and caddisfly larvae. But the individuals tend to be larger.

Most mayfly nymphs in runs are large and blocky crawlers, although the exceptions include the smallest of the mayfly species: the White-Winged Curses, or Tricos, as we call them now. But if you want to interest a two-pound trout holding along the bottom of a run in a mayfly nymphal imitation, it had better be a number twelve rather than a number twenty-four.

The caddis of runs are also larger and include a mix of both free-living and case-building types. Again, there are tiny representatives of the order, but if you want a large trout to find and wallop your fly, it should be at least a number twelve unless there is a hatch going on that advises you otherwise.

Runs are home to the largest of the stoneflies, which are almost the largest of the aquatic insects. Giant salmon fly nymphs live in their thousands in the broken water of fast runs. They are considered by many to be the most important single hatch of the year. But their importance, from the view of the trout, is not confined to their late-spring hatch period. Salmon flies and other large stoneflies have three-year life cycles; the nymphs of the early year-classes are out in the runs, available to trout, all year long. They are a staple in the diet, down along the bottom, throughout all the seasons.

Salmon fly nymphs are typical of the trout foods in runs.

Trout do not go hungry in runs, but they do tend to feed less often, on bigger bites.

Crayfish are common among the larger rocks of runs. They are scavengers, living on both plant and animal life, whatever they can catch in their claws. They forage most when the light is dim, and through the night. Trout come out to hunt them down whenever they can find them, but most often it's at dawn and dusk.

Sculpins are more at home in runs than in riffles. They are bottom-huggers, living right down against the stones, invisible against them except when they move. Though I have no evidence to prove it, I suspect that trout sometimes nose around their territories like hunters after pheasants, flushing sculpins and gunning them down on the wing.

Other baitfish, and trout fingerlings, forage in schools along the edges of runs. They are one of the major reasons that large trout move out of their prime lies to hunt in the shallows, especially when the light is low.

Temperature and Oxygen

Runs offer excellent temperature and oxygen regimes in all but the most stressful conditions. A stream has to be on the brink of disaster before trout will find any benefit by moving out of runs and into highly oxygenated riffles. Such conditions do occur; in some damaged or desert watersheds they happen almost annually. But most of the time trout maintain their stations in runs even in hot weather.

When conditions do become extreme, many of the springheads that cool a stream are found in runs. Wherever a side stream makes its entrance in a run, you can expect to find fish holding in the cooler water just downstream.

TYPES OF RUNS

There are four basic types of runs: barren runs, feeding runs, holding runs, and prime runs.

Barren runs have little life in them, at least of the kind that makes them attractive to trout. The most common kind of run that lacks life is a run that has no sort of rock or rubble on its bottom or else has a bottom of stones that are so small and uniform that they do not form lies where trout can hold against the current.

If a run has a silt or sand bottom it will not have a great deal of insect life unless it has lots of rotted vegetation. But freestone runs are subject to scour, and vegetation seldom gets a chance to take root. A featureless run does not have many places where a trout can get shelter from the current. Because a smooth bottom means a glassy surface, there will be little protection from overhead predation.

The only kind of silt- or sand-bottomed run that is rich is one with a growth of rooted aquatic vegetation. But any run that is slow enough, shallow enough, and safe enough from winter scour to allow the growth of vegetation suffers in this book from the sin of getting itself classified as a *flat* and is discussed in Chapter 8.

Another kind of barren run is the long and slow and turbid kind found in the lower reaches of major rivers. These might have rocky bottoms, but in most cases the rocks are so covered with silt that there are few places left for insects to live. The water is often opaque; sunlight does not penetrate to the bottom. Photosynthesis could not take place if a bit of algal growth could find a clean stone to stand on.

Feeding runs are rare. You won't encounter them on many streams, but I have fished a few. Trout do not hold on them, but they move up into them whenever a hatch is on. These runs are shallow, two feet deep or less. Some are fast, bordering on riffles. Others are slow, bordering on flats. Most are studded with stones, and have plenty of shelter from the current. They have good insect populations. But they offer very poor protection from predators.

Most runs of this kind are braided around boulders of about basketball size and smaller, many with their tops protruding out of water. These would form holding lies if the water were deeper and the current less steady. But in this kind of water the surface is an open window. Only small trout will hold in the exposed positions it offers.

My experience in this kind of water has been that attached algae grows from the stones, waving downstream in longer beards as summer wears on. This attached algae is a hotbed for insect growth, and also harbors great numbers of crustaceans such as scuds and cress bugs.

Fish nose up into feeding runs whenever a food form is active and conning trout into risking aerial predation. When the source of food disappears, trout will move out of these kinds of runs to water where they can find protection from predators.

Holding runs offer trout shelter from currents and protection from predators, but they are not rich in opportunities to feed. This does not mean that trout merely hold in them and nap until they move out into a feeding run to stock up. A holding run delivers food down its currents and trout hold their stations, defending their territories from intruders, feeding on what washes their way. They do not leave their lies unless enticed out of them by an abundance of food in some other kind of water nearby.

Most holding runs are two to four feet in depth and fairly homogeneous in their bottom structure. If anything defines them, it is a lack of rooted or attached vegetation and a scarcity of spaces between rocks for insects to hide and grow. Often these types of runs have sandy or slightly silted bottoms with stones that are embedded into the finer substrate. Rocks entrenched this way deflect the current, forming lies. But bottoms like these don't produce much trout food.

Holding runs always hold trout. But the size of the trout, regardless of the size of the territory, is dictated by the amount of food available nearby. As Charlie Brooks said in *The Trout and the Stream*, "It is true that the larger the fish the larger volume of water he requires, but first he requires sufficient *food* to make him large." Most trout found in holding runs will be from small to average in size. Large fish will not remain in them for long periods of time unless there is a dependable and prolific source of food very near them.

Prime runs are what we think about when we clasp our hands behind our heads, lean back in our winter chairs, and daydream about *trout water.* These runs combine the aspects of feeding and holding runs: they contain lots of prime lies that fulfill all of the needs of the trout in one spot. They have sprinklings of boulders to give shelter from currents. They are usually three to six feet deep, providing plenty of protection from predators. Most important, they have bottoms of clean stones in mixed sizes: there are lots of living rooms for insects and a thin but rich layer of algal growth to feed them so they can grow and be happy and feed the fish.

The larger bottom features in prime runs also provide shelter for other organisms: crayfish and baitfish and even some sinuous and nasty leeches live wherever the water is slow enough. Big trout thrive on these big bites and find that they don't ever have to leave their territories to get any of their basic needs met.

HOLDING LIES IN RUNS

Reading runs to locate prime lies is more critical than it is in riffles. Trout are less scattered; they hold where combinations of food and security are as good as they can find according to their size. Where the water is prime they establish stations that are fairly close together, though each gives a window onto a separate territory.

The territorial imperative declines as the water slows. In very slow runs trout almost bunch up. This tendency to gather in the best water is the reason you sometimes fish through most of a run without getting a bump, then suddenly hook fish after fish in a limited pocket. It happened to me on a run in a river in Montana last year.

The river was medium-sized, about two casts wide. It alternated between long riffles and short runs. I fished a riffle with a wet fly. The water was shallow and sunlit and rich, but there were few holding lies in it and I coaxed no trout to my fly. I moved down to the run below, but didn't change from the downstream wet-fly strategy I'd tried fruitlessly above.

The head of the run, where the riffle broke into it, looked good. But no fish moved to my fly there. I fished around a few boulders, where the water promised fish, but the promises were not

The author lands a rainbow hooked in a prime trout run fed by a small riffle at its head. (*photo by Jim Schollmeyer*)

fulfilled. Finally I waded into the center of the run – it was only about three feet deep – and began casting alternately to both banks. I worked along for about fifty feet this way without a tap. Then my fly began to work an arc that carried it toward the edge of a patch of shade dropped from a pine tree leaning precariously from the left bank.

When the fly skirted the darkness cast by the tree a fish came out and rapped it. It was a brown, about fourteen inches long. I played it, netted it, released it. I cast again to the same place and again a fish went *whap.*

The length of run flowing through the shadow of the tree was no more than twenty feet. In that short distance I took no fewer than fifteen trout, all between twelve and sixteen inches long. Some were browns, some were rainbows. All were fine fish, and all held in the shade. When I fished through it and beyond it I got no more strikes.

On an impulse I decided to wade back up through the shade to shore, to get out and take a rest. But just outside the shadows the bottom began to get away from me. I tried to wade through, but before I reached the area that held the fish the water was trying to tickle my armpits. I had to back out of there and go down and around the shadow to reach shore.

Since I didn't recognize that pocket until I almost fell into it, since I did not go right to it and fish it immediately upon arriving at the run, what business have I got writing a book about reading water? It's a good question. The only answer I have is that I did discern the most likely holding areas in the run, and did fish them one at a time until I stumbled onto the one that held trout.

By learning to recognize high-percentage lies, and by fishing them one at a time, we eventually stumble into a piece of water that produces fish. Held in that regard, it's not really a stumble. *Movement is a major element of a successful fly-fishing strategy.*

Though it is a minor digression to say it here, the same thing is true of tactics. The angler who tries this, then that, and finally the other thing, will, if he can keep things to a level just under a frenzy, have fun and eventually find a tactic that takes trout. To an observer it might look like an accident. It is not: Change is another of the major elements of a successful fly-fishing strategy.

Head of a Run

The riffle above a run delivers an almost constant supply of drift. The head of a run, with its corner pockets filled like the cheeks of a chipmunk, are second in productivity only to the corners of riffles. Sometimes they are not even second.

The richness of the riffle above is the direct cause for the productivity of the head of a run. One does well to glance at the riffle that feeds into any run; it is a part of assessing the potential of the run. A brief and bouldered riffle will produce insects, but not as many as a long and pebbled one where the water bounces down whitely, so thin and fast no trout could hold in it to pick over the current's offerings before they get delivered to the run below.

The productivity of the head of a run is also based on its potential as holding water. If it forms as a chute with little to break the current, there will be few places for trout to hold and they will move into the head of the run as they do into a feeding riffle: only when there is such an abundance of food that it makes fighting the current worth the energy expended. If the head of the run has a relatively slow current with gentle eddies off to the sides, trout will establish territories and stick to their stations.

If the head of the run shelves off immediately into fairly deep water, from four to six feet, it is very likely to be a prime lie. This kind of lie located immediately below a long productive riffle can hold the largest trout in the stream. Trout often stack up there; they find shelter from currents, protection from predators, and an abundant supply of feed. A small territory is sufficient. It is the kind of lie where you can take your limit without moving your feet, if you are interested in taking a limit.

Obstructions in Runs

The next most likely place to find fish in a run is around any visible obstruction along its length. The obstruction that first leaps to mind is a midstream boulder. It attracts trout for the same reason it would in a riffle: anything that breaks the current provides shelter from it and makes a likely holding lie. If the water around it is deep enough to provide protection from predators, the lie creeps quickly toward the prime class.

A large boulder in the current provides more than just a single

Fishing over a boulder that is marked only by a boil.

holding lie. The pillow of water just upstream is often overlooked but is often the most productive water. It is a good lie for a trout, a comfortable station with an unblocked window on the current. It is also the easiest water to fish around a boulder. A dry fly cast two or three feet upstream, with lots of slack tossed into the leader, will drift down to it naturally. A weighted nymph cast five to fifteen feet upstream, depending on the strength of the current and its depth, will sink down and tumble right into the pillow before it is drawn off to the side by the water that breaks around the boulder.

There are slight delta-winged eddies at each side of a midstream boulder. The current gets busy like a whisk broom and hollows out small depressions at the base of each wing, right down under the edge of the boulder. The current delivers bits of food that swirl into the eddies. Trout hold there. The problem is the difficulty in delivering a fly to them. The tug of the line, caught in the current between yourself and the boulder, draws the fly out almost every time. About the only way to defeat this is to wade very close, lob a heavily weighted bomb, and fish it down right underneath your rod top.

The storied big-fish lie in almost all fishing fables is the eddied water behind a big boulder in a deep and dark run. The reason is simple: this kind of water holds lots of fish, sometimes very big ones. They hold in the interrupted water behind the rock, closer to it than is commonly recognized.

The water immediately behind an obstruction is almost still. A few feet downstream, water that has separated and swung wide around each side of the rock gets back together and noses upstream to see what went wrong. The result is a turbulence that is not pillowing, but a confusing type that tosses the fish around. They like to hold in this kind of turbulence about as much as I like to fly through thunderstorms in my brother's six-seat Cessna.

That does not mean trout do not hold downstream from mid-stream boulders. The opposite is true: they hold close in behind the boulder and they also hold in the eddied water downstream a few feet from it, but *right along the bottom,* beneath the confused water.

Taking trout from lies behind boulders has been, and still is, a problem for me. I do not have the kind of success fishing behind boulders that literature predicts I should. I must be doing something wrong because it's unlikely that the trout are.

I have my best luck if the run is relatively shallow, two to four feet deep, and the fish are willing to rise up for dry flies. It's difficult to get a decent drift in the eddy behind a boulder. I try to keep the dry bouncing on the water immediately behind it. A fish gets a bit of a chance to see the fly and will usually slash up quickly if it's going to rise at all.

Your line wants to pull the fly out to the sides, or downstream, creating almost immediate drag. Hold your rod as high as you can. This extends the float of the fly. The closer you wade, the shorter you cast, and the more line you lift off the water, the better your chance of keeping the fly dancing where you want it until it goads a strike.

The same problems apply when trying to get a nymph down to the fish. The nymph has to plummet like a stone if it is to get down before it gets washed out of the holding water. It helps to use very heavily weighted flies. It also helps to wade as close as you can, cast short, and hold your rod high. You will have a problem detecting takes even with a strike indicator because the confusing currents tug the indicator in all directions.

Always fish out the eddied water for a few feet downstream from the boulder after you have probed the water immediately below it. Fish either on the surface or right on the bottom; there is little mid-depth fishing in this kind of water.

Other kinds of obstructions should be fished like midstream boulders. A log or a root wad lodged in a run offers the same kind of cover a boulder provides. They are nastier to fish because you are more likely to get snagged. But the trout will be down under the obstruction and you'll have to do your best to get your flies to them without getting hung in the wood.

Generally, the larger the obstruction in a run the larger the fish it will shelter. But the size of the object has to be related to the depth of the run: a two-foot-deep run with a boulder the size of a Buick protruding out of it will not hold the same size trout as a six-foot-deep run obstructed by a boulder the size of a beach ball.

Look for large fish where the water looks like it would provide for them. In some ways, and with lots of experience, reading water boils down to something almost as simple as that.

Invisible Obstructions

Boils on the surface reflect boulders below. These lies are as prime as visible boulders, perhaps more so because their depth adds concealment and protects trout more thoroughly from predation. The first thing to do with an invisible boulder is figure out exactly where it rests on the bottom. You want to fish the boulder, not the boil.

A boulder will be from a foot to about five feet upstream from its boil, depending on the depth and speed of the current. Once you have placed it, spend a moment imagining it in your mind. Picture it with its pillow in front of it, its little winged eddies out to the side, its eddied water close downstream. Put fish in all these places, in your mind. Once you have envisioned it in this way, fish it exactly as if it protruded above the water and you could see every feature the current created.

Trenches and Shelves

Runs tend to have a lot more shelving water than do riffles because they work their way to base rock more often. In some runs, trenches are the primary features, and you don't hook trout until you run a fly down through them.

You can usually spot a trench by the slightly darker water on the surface above it. But it would be dishonest to predict that all of them can be spied this way. There are excellent runs that you can only scope by wading and feeling for them. It's best to do this kind of exploration by probing with a wading staff, unless you don't mind buffaloing downstream in pursuit of a floating hat.

Anybody who knows how to read water can approach a run with visible trenches and figure out how to find the fish. But rivers with runs that have invisible trenches, shelves, and ledges are the kinds of rivers that produce best for somebody on the home team. You've got to know these kinds of rivers to fish them at their best.

Any book on reading water would be missing some sentences if it didn't point out the advantages of fishing water that you've fished over and over. You learn where the fish hold by having a history of where you've caught them before. You know where some lies are by a history of having stepped into them before. By owning a home river, or being owned by one, you not only learn its lies, you learn more about the characteristics of all lies. Everything you learn on your own river will go with you to any river you ever fish.

Back to trenches and shelves.

If a trench is etched into the bottom parallel to the flow, you should fish carefully down the length of it. Work a dry fly over its surface. Cast wets so they swim across the top of it, a couple of feet farther downstream on each successive cast. Drop nymphs so they sink and tumble along the bottom of it.

Where a shelf is cut across the current, the result is a sudden deepening that both breaks the flow and creates a vertical eddy in it. Trout hang in the water just below the shelf. They enjoy the depth, the ease, and the churning of insects that eases over the lip and swirls into the eddy. In this kind of situation you should present dry flies so they ride the currents just below the shelf, bouncing on top of the eddy. Nymphs should be cast upstream from the shelf and then be allowed to wash down with the current, free-drift, to drop over the shelf just as a dislodged natural nymph or larva would appear to the trout.

Any deepening in the water of a run, whether it is caused by a shelving trench, a depression etched out in a gravel bottom, or a natural and gradual narrowing and deepening of the river, should be considered potential holding water. Trout make stations in all such water, holding on territories or moving out to forage if there is not a sufficient amount of feed there to fuel them. These depths will be revealed in some cases by the darkness of the water, in other cases by a slick on the surface. In many cases they will not be revealed at all, and you will have to know your river to know about them.

Whichever clue you read, fish trenches and shelves carefully, because they hold some of the nicest trout any stream offers its anglers.

Current Seams

The joining of any conflicting currents provides a potential feeding lie in a run, just as it does in a riffle. Some seams in runs are easier to spot because the surface is not as choppy and a couple of prominent currents will meet in obvious conflict. But other seams are difficult to spot. Two gentle and slow currents coming together meld without much disturbance and you will have to look carefully to see the line where they meet.

One way to recognize the convergence of two currents is to notice the things that divide them in the first place. Sometimes it is then obvious where they naturally rejoin downstream.

An example is an island. Where one splits the flow there is usually a triangle of quiet water at its downstream point. Fish of much size will not hold in this quiet water unless it is three feet deep or more. But the apex of the triangle of quiet water points straight downstream to the seam where the two currents that

Slight riffle at the upper end causes a seam of slightly choppier water that runs the length of a run.

went around opposite sides of the island get together again. This seam gathers insects and drift from both currents and causes considerable fallout of feed all along its length.

You should drift your dry flies down the seam and along both sides of it. If you are fishing wets, cast them and retrieve them so they swing across the seam. Nymphs should be tumbled the length of the seam, down on the bottom, where fish feed on the fallout.

Other seams occur in runs where currents of two different speeds come together. The two speeds can be caused by a riffle that delivers the water in two or three tendrils. It can also be caused by different depths somewhere in the run, with the water over each depth flowing at a different rate. These are the hardest seams to read, but they do have their indications.

The surface of the water on one side or the other might be a bit rougher. An eddy line, barely perceptible, might swirl for a few feet before the currents have commingled enough to average their speeds. If the reason for the difference in speeds is a difference in depth, a darkening might show on one side. Such seams are doubly desirable because they not only gather feed from both currents but offer the advantage of shelving water and better protection beneath the water. Fish these seams like any others, but be sure to get your nymphs down to the bottom of the deepest water if trout refuse to come up for drys.

The most common kinds of seams are those where a run flows through a field of protruding boulders. The current splits and rejoins. It goes fast this way and slow that way. The speeds must meld. Several rocks in staggered rows bounce the currents around and cause several seams. They are all potential holding lies and should be fished carefully.

Shade

I mentioned shade as a kind of holding cover. It becomes more of a factor on flats, where it might be the only kind of cover around in shallow water. In runs, shade is usually important only in conjunction with some other factor.

When I took fifteen trout out of twenty feet of water on that Montana river, it seemed at first that shade was the only reason they held there. But when I tried to wade to shore and discovered the water was suddenly deeper, it became apparent that the cause was the combination of shade and deeper water. It was a nice set of circumstances for the trout on a bright day, and they gathered there from all the rest of the run.

Tailout of a Run

Some runs make an exit by slowing and lifting over a buildup of gravel. The bottom is almost always uniform in nature, without boulders or other obstructions to the gathering current. The water is shallow, lacking substantial protection from predators. But this transitional water is usually rich in aquatic insect life.

Rick Hafele fishing the slick tailout of a broad run.

The tailout of a run is an excellent feeding lie. Trout materialize out of nowhere to feed hungrily whenever a hatch comes off.

It is difficult water to fish. The surface is usually glassy, the current too swift to wade easily, and the fish spooky. You can't get as close to the fish as you would like to; you can't get good drifts with medium-to-long casts. Because the trout have usually arrived at the invitation of a specific species of insect, you've got to match the hatch in order to attract their interest.

I have had my best luck fishing big and pushy tailouts with wet flies that approximate the size and color of whatever natural is hatching. It is easier to present a wet in a natural manner, drifting across a tailout, than it is to get a plausible presentation with a dry fly.

Dry-fly fishing can be superb on shallow and gentle tailouts. You will want to stalk the fish, pinpoint their rises, and present your flies right down their feeding lanes. Because the water is thin and usually clear, you don't want to line the fish. Approach from upstream, cast down at a quartering angle, and feed slack to your fly so it drifts downstream without apparent attachment.

The evident lies in a run, from its head to its tailout, are all places to pinpoint your fishing. All of the different kinds of holding water have the potential to turn up concentrations of trout. Knowing how to read the various water types will help you locate a concentration more quickly.

It is also possible that trout might hold on invisible lies, scattered throughout the water as they often are in riffles. When this is the case it works best to set up a disciplined casting pattern, covering most of the potential holding water in the run.

TACTICS FOR FISHING RUNS

Trout can be moody in runs. In riffles they tend always to be feeding actively or at least seem to be willing to accept something that passes in the drift. The activity of trout in runs is more closely tied to the activity of what they eat. If aquatic insects are on the move trout will be moving, too. If nothing is happening, trout tend to hold on their stations, resting, perhaps feeding a bit when an opportunity presents itself.

When this is the case, they are willing to take the convenient bit of food – or the artificial fly – that arrives to them on the drift. But they are less willing to move far for it. If you are fishing the bottom, you will have to be sure your fly is right down there. No matter what you use – nymph, wet, or dry – you will have to cover the water carefully with it to be sure that it comes close to the trout on at least one of its passes.

When they are truly dour you've almost got to hit them on the nose, which is not easy. But most of the time, that is not the case; you've just got to get the fly within a foot or two of them. Since runs hold so many trout, once you've found the right kind of water you should have no trouble getting your fly within striking range of at least a few of them.

When a specific species of insect is active – emerging or making its way to the surface to emerge – trout in runs tend to key on them. The surface is not choppy like that of a riffle; trout get a better look at your fly. They are more likely to reject a poor imitation and are almost certain to reject a fly presented in an unrealistic manner.

When considering fishing tactics for runs, the same three levels apply: the bottom, mid-depths, and top. The three levels tend to be more distinct in runs; the bottom is farther from the top, and the mid-depth area is more of a distinct region between the two. Trout feeding in a riffle can cover all the levels while holding on the bottom. They are usually willing to move to anything that drifts near them, at any of the levels. In a run, trout feeding at one level might refuse to respond to a fly fished at any other level.

Tackle for Fishing Runs

Again I would like to mourn the lack of a caddy. Without one it is advantageous to carry a rod that fishes well in a wide variety of water types, rather than one that fishes well in only one narrow set of circumstances.

The best rod for fishing riffles, examined in the last chapter, seems to be an eight-and-one-half to nine-footer balanced to cast a five-weight line. You will want to toss some larger and heavier flies in runs. If you were willing to trot back to the car, you would probably return to the water with the same length rod balanced to cast a six- or seven-weight line. But if you are like me you don't like to trot in waders.

The best thing to do when you leave the car is to select a rod that is properly suited to the size of the stream, *not* the particular water types within it. You will want to fish all of the water types in the course of a day, unless you get rooted to one damn fine spot. The right outfit will let you do it.

I have already divided the world into creeks, streams, and rivers. I use a seven-foot four-weight rod on creeks, an eight-foot five-weight on streams, an eight-and-a-half-foot six-weight on rivers. I routinely find myself wishing that my rod was a half foot longer and a line-size heavier. I specifically recommend that you use a seven-and-a-half-foot number-five for creeks, an eight-and-a-half-foot number-six for streams, and a nine-foot number-seven for rivers. I also recommend that you use what you like.

Personality has more to do with rod selection than any of us would like to admit. Your rod choice will work better for you if it suits your personality, not mine.

Most fishing in runs, at least most of mine, can still be accomplished with a double-taper dry line. I like the control it gives. Tending the drift of the fly can be more important in a run than it is in a riffle. But I don't think anybody would suffer greatly from using a weight-forward line. That's what most modern and progressive folks use. Its biggest disadvantage would be the temptation to cast too far with it. You will always catch more trout if you keep your casts as short as you can.

The one major addition to your tackle vest, for fishing runs, should be a spare reel spool holding a wet-tip line with a fairly fast but not super-fast sink rate. It will get your nymphs down into the deepest parts of runs. Without one, there will be places you just can't fish effectively. But don't go to the wet-tip if you can get down deep enough with the dry line and some weight on the leader. It's easier to fish, and easier to detect takes, with the floating line and a strike indicator.

The leader should start out about the length of the rod. Add a couple of feet of tippet to suit the flies you will be casting, and it should be just right. If you get into a hatch and find fish selective to something small, you will want to add some finer tippet, which will also make the leader longer, which is the perfect way to respond to the increased fussiness of the fish without getting the situation confused by complicated leader formulae.

When fishing dry flies or wets in runs, a three- or four-pound leader seems about right. Extend it with two-pound-test if you must match a hatch. Stiffen it to six- or eight-pound-test for nymphing deep; let this depend on the size of the flies you want to cast and the weight of the fish you hope to take.

If you switch to the wet-tip line, shorten your leader to four or five feet. Trout are not leader-shy when feeding on the bottom. It doesn't make sense to use a sinking line to get your fly to the bottom, only to have a long fine leader buoy it back up.

Fishing the Bottom of a Run

Trout in runs, holding as they do along the bottom when they are not feeding, are less likely to move all the way up to the surface to take dry flies. That is why nymphs are more effective as searching patterns, especially in water more than four feet deep. The bottom is the most promising level to start fishing in a run because that is where trout spend most of their time.

Your fly selection should be related to the predominant natural foods. Usually mayfly nymphs or caddisfly larvae will be most abundant. The same Gold-Ribbed Hare's Ear, Gray Nymph, or Zug Bug that worked in a riffle will usually work on the bottom of a run, though it should be tied on a number eight, ten, or twelve hook.

If there are stonefly populations in the run, a large and heavily weighted salmon-fly-nymph pattern will work better. The Box Canyon Stone in size six or eight is a good place to start. Bitch Creek Nymphs and Yuk Bugs, with their funny-looking rubber legs, look less like the real thing, but seem somehow able to con more trout on big western waters. It doesn't look good on a trout's

Typical set-up for nymphing the bottom of a run.

resume to get caught on something so ugly. But it's smart for us to fish with what works, and we don't plan to hire them anyway.

If one of these general dressings doesn't work, you should do a little collecting by plucking stones off the bottom. It is more efficient to collect with an aquatic insect net, holding it against the bottom and kicking at stones upstream from it. But I don't carry a collecting net most of the time and suspect you don't either. I prefer to reserve my scientific sampling for specific situations, for example on the occasions I am forced to fish fine over trout rising on flats.

Once you've chosen a fly, you will need to choose between the dry and wet-tip lines. My simple rule for all fishing is this: Fish a dry line until conditions demand that you use something else. Don't use the wet-tip unless you can't reach the bottom with the dry line and a reasonable amount of weight on the leader. But switch without hesitation if your fly isn't fishing down where you want it.

In most cases you won't need the wet-tip until the water is more than five feet deep, which is deeper than you can wade comfortably unless you're a lot taller than I am. But if the current is strong, a wet-tip can be an advantage in water as shallow as three feet deep.

To fish the bottom of most runs, the best presentation technique is the upstream dead drift. Use a weighted nymph and add weight to the leader when needed, which will be most of the time. Place the strike indicator twice the depth of the water above the fly. Cast short, twenty to thirty feet, and let your fly sink to the bottom as it drifts down toward you. Raise the rod and draw in slack line as the fly approaches; lower the rod and feed out slack as the fly departs downstream. When it has reached the end of its drift, lift it up and lob it back upstream, a foot or two out from the line of the last drift. Set the hook at any hesitation of the indicator.

When you have fished out the part of the run you can reach with an easy cast, move upstream five to ten feet and repeat the process.

This method is deadly when fishing the prime holding lies of a run. You can place the fly right in on top of the fish. You have excellent control, so that you can work the fly into the best water.

This is especially important when working around boulders, the most common type of prime holding lie in a run.

Another method for fishing the bottom of a run works well where the water is fairly slow and not more than about four feet deep. It does not work if the water is either deep or swift. It calls for a wet-tip line and a large nymph or streamer. Otherwise it is similar to the wet-fly tactics described in the last chapter, though there can be a substantial difference in the kind of fish you catch.

The first part of this strategy calls for wading into position, in reference to a prime lie, so that you can cast slightly upstream from straight across and let the fly drift down toward it. Quickly toss mends into the drift so the line tip and fly sink without hindrance. The first twenty feet or so of the drift should be dead. By the time the fly is at a forty-five-degree angle downstream from you, it should be near the bottom and sweeping into the prime lie. Your line should pick it up at this point and begin to tug it across the stream. The idea is to keep it down as deep as you can while drawing it slowly around until it is straight below you.

I used this strategy once while fishing the Williamson River with rascallious Polly Rosborough, author of *Tying and Fishing the Fuzzy Nymphs*. Polly was then celebrating his eighty-first birthday. He fished a few hours, finished up in a short run, then sat on a log to take a short rest. I caught up with him and asked for the honor of taking a few casts with his rod. He allowed it.

The rod was armed with a wet-tip line, short leader, and large but unweighted nymph of Polly's own devising. So far as I know, the fly never did reach the stage of development where in his opinion it deserved a name.

The run was about fifty feet wide, an even four feet deep, and no more than seventy-five feet long. I waded ten feet out, near the head of it, to work downstream. I kept my casts to about forty feet, placing each on the water a bit upstream from my position in the run. I tossed mends into each cast until the fly was as deep as I could get it. Then I fished it around. Between casts I took two or three steps, letting the current push me down. I didn't fish any particular lie because all of the water looked good.

I'd taken only about ten casts, was still getting used to the feel of Polly's rod, when I felt a thud. The fish came up and tumbled once in the air, then fought sullenly along the bottom. I did not encourage it to come up again; I had seen it and was afraid I might lose it. When it finally tired out and came to my hands, I estimated its weight somewhere between five and six pounds before releasing it. It was a privilege to catch it on the famous man's rod.

There is another way to cover the deep ground in runs. It is usually used on the big rivers of the West: the Yellowstone below the park, the Missouri between dams, and other rivers of slightly smaller caliber. This method calls for casting with thirty-foot shooting heads of super-fast-sinking line, backed by a hundred feet of Cobra or Amnesia monofilament, flung by nine- and ten-foot rods in the nine- and ten-weight class. The ammunition is large streamers: sizes two through four Woolly Buggers, Spruce Flies, or Muddlers, all weighted till they go *thud* when dropped into your palm.

The presentation method is simple: wade deep, cast long and slightly upstream, allow some time for the fly to plummet, then let the line tighten against the fly and lead it on around. Sometimes the fly is activated with a pulsed rod tip; sometimes it is allowed to swing around with only the action given to it by the current. This method can be brutal to those not used to casting long with big gear. But it subdues many of the largest trout that are taken each season.

Tactics for Fishing Mid-depths

Fishing mid-depths in runs should be a tactic reserved for those times when insect activity dictates it. When caddis pupae or mayfly nymphs are on the move from bottom to top, trout in runs sometimes feed on them in between. More often even these are taken just as they leave the bottom or when they reach the barrier of the surface film. Except in rare circumstances, the mid-depths are barren water in a run. Unfortunately, it is the very water that many people fish ninety percent of the time—one of the reasons they only catch ten percent of the trout.

But it helps to know how to fish the mid-depth level when trout are feeding there. The tactics are largely those described for fishing the same water in riffles. Fish wet flies or small nymphs

Fishing a shallow run with a few visible features.

from upstream, letting them swing slowly around on the current, mending the line to slow the fly and achieve some depth. Or fish slightly weighted nymphs upstream, using a strike indicator placed about twice the depth you want to fish your fly.

But I don't want to dwell on methods for fishing runs at mid-depths. It's a kind of fishing you should be led to by some sort of insect activity. The tactic you select should then be based on what the insects and the trout are doing. Whether you use a wet fly or a nymph, you should present the fly in a manner that makes it arrive in front of the trout the same way the active natural would.

Tactics for Fishing the Surface

The top is also a zone where you will do your best when trout can be seen actively rising. The surface is smoother in runs, and trout tend to be at least slightly more selective than they are in riffles. Your choice of fly pattern and presentation should be based on what the hatch of the moment requires. Again, rather than going into detail and doubling the length of this already long chapter, I will refer you to *Handbook of Hatches,* which covers identification, fly pattern selection, and presentation methods in detail for all of the aquatic insect hatches.

In runs from two to four feet deep, trout can often be brought to the surface when there is little or no insect activity. You can enjoy some success fishing the dry fly without waiting for signs of rising fish. I call this *searching* fishing, and enjoy it a great deal. I enjoy it more, in fact, than nymph fishing down on the bottom. But the latter is apt to be more productive than the former, and catching fish on nymphs can be more fun than not catching fish on dry flies.

Certain kinds of runs predict the success of the searching dry fly. They are generally shallow and broken with boulders, visible or invisible, that form scattered holding lies in which trout feed opportunistically. If the stream is narrow and forested, the chance of terrestrial activity on the water is increased, and trout are more likely to be alert for opportunities that arrive on the surface. In late summer, hoppers and other terrestrials cause trout to look upward in meadow streams.

Fishing runs with dry flies can be done with the same dressings used on riffles: the Elk Hair Caddis, Royal Wulff, Humpy, and various traditional dressings such as the Adams and Light Cahill in sizes ten and twelve. Meaty attractor drys seem best when you have to draw trout up through several feet of water.

Presentation techniques for dry flies in runs are not any news. In most cases you can fish upstream casts without fear of frightening the fish. Curb your casts so you can control the drift of the fly and keep it from dragging on the surface. The farther off you fish, the more chance the line and leader will cross unseen conflicting currents, causing the fly to move unnaturally but so subtly that you don't even notice it. The trout will.

If the run is particularly smooth on top, you might find it advantageous to fish casts that are almost straight out from you, mending and tending the line so you get a long free drift of the fly. This keeps the line and leader from crossing the fish before the fly reaches it. It is an exceptionally good tactic for stalking pinpointed prime lies, presenting your casts to the most likely holding water in the run.

7

Anatomy of a Pool

Show a fisherman a likely lie and he will declare, "That's a nice looking pool!" It might be a riffle or a run, but if it looks like it might hold trout, it is automatically called a *pool*. Perhaps this terminology is not mistaken. But to make a book about reading water work, a pool must have its own definition, separate from riffles and runs and other water types that hold trout.

A pool is a reach of stream where the water slows nearly to stillness and deepens compared to the water above and below it.

True pools—bodies of deep slow water, not just any water that looks like it would hold a trout—are largely passed up by fly fishermen, especially on big rivers, because they are the most difficult water to fish. But they offer the biggest fish in any stream and are worth the effort it takes to get to know them.

STRUCTURE OF A POOL

A pool varies in size, obviously, with the size of the stream that forms it. A pool in a mountain headwater creek might be ten feet

long, five feet wide, and just three or four feet deep. Not large, but certainly large enough to give rest and comfort to the size fish found in a creek that hurries off a hillside. Some pools in the Big Hole River, on the other hand, cannot be cast across. They might be a hundred yards long, half that wide, and ten to twelve feet deep. And they hold trout that suit their sizes.

A pool, small or large, is the slowest and deepest water in the stream it's in. The other water types, upstream and down, are faster and shallower. A pool need not be a sudden drop in the stream's bottom. But if the bottom were a line drawn down through the course of riffles and runs and flats, a pool would be a distinct dip and rise along that line.

The structure of a typical pool is simple: it has a head where the water enters, a body that deepens and darkens, and a tailout where the water lifts and shallows out again to break over into

the next water type. There are as many variations as there are typical pools, but most pools have the same three parts in one shape or another: head, body, and tailout.

Some pools are long and deep. They would be runs if the water were not so slow, almost lacking a defining current. Others are short, abrupt, dropping straight off into deep water, taking a turn or two around it, then shallowing up to speed on downstream again.

Pools are most common in creeks and streams that are still up in the hills, eroding their way into immature streamcourses, trying to subdue the land. Some of the substrate over which they flow is more resistant than others. There's lots of bedrock, and the stream has dug lots of holes in it. All of the stone hasn't been ground into boulders and rocks and pebbles yet, so there isn't much material to shove around, to fill in the holes, to even things out as they are lower down in the stream system. A mature river, flowing across flat land, has lots of deep runs but few true pools.

The head of a pool usually has some rubble and rock tumbled into it from the riffle or run above. This makes fairly good habitat for aquatic insects; it is similar in structure to the bottom of a run, and the insects that live there tend to be larger types, like those in a run.

The bottom structure of the body of a pool depends largely on the kind of stream it is in. A lot of them are scoured to bedrock. The finest sediment is deposited wherever the water is slowest, so pools that aren't worked to bedrock tend to have bottoms that lack cobble and therefore lack the crowding of small spaces that aquatic insects love. Instead, pool bottoms are often littered with larger rocks and boulders. These provide fewer but much larger spaces. As you would suspect, larger beasts tend to live there.

The tailout of a pool is similar to the tailout of a run. It is a buildup of small pebbles and stones, with some larger cobble. Unless the stream lacks vigor, the tailout gathers speed as it lifts up, and this increase of flow keeps the tailout cleansed of silt. The stones are as clean as those found in a riffle. Sunlight strikes down to them, increasing photosynthetic growth. Tailouts are excellent habitat for the same kinds of smaller aquatic insects that live in riffles.

THE NEEDS OF TROUT

Pools meet all of the needs of trout in ways that make them satisfying to the very largest fish found in a given stream. They are the cream of prime lies. If you are after the largest trout of your life, pools should rise to the top of your list of places to fish.

Shelter from Currents

Pools offer the maximum in terms of shelter from abusive currents. The water is slow; in its depths there are places where it does not require much energy at all for a trout to hold its station, at least when water flow is normal.

Shelter from currents becomes a live-or-die situation during winter spate and spring runoff. Trout find shelter as near their home lies as they can, but there is sometimes little available. When conditions are extreme, many trout are pushed into pools. Perhaps that is why nature, with her patient wisdom, turns down the territorial instinct as the water gets slower. Trout can gather in shelter that way with fewer quarrels and less stress in an already stressful situation.

Protection from Predators

The need for protection from predators is met in pools by depth and its companion, darkness. Trout are secure there from aerial predation.

They are not entirely secure from the likes of mergansers and otters. But safety is relative; trout are safer in a deep pool than they are in a run where the light is better, as is the chance for surprise.

The darkness at the bottom of a pool often makes it the best bomb shelter around. It is where trout flee when danger looms. But fish do not come double-timing in battalions from distant lies. A trout on a long flat will not flee the length of it to bury its head in a pool. It will have its hide nearer home, though it might not be as good. But a pool adjacent to a flat or a riffle might be sanctuary for many of the fish that have lies in the nearby shallow water.

Trout Foods in Pools

The need for food is met in pools in the form of the biggest bites. Riffles offer a constant supply of small insects to trout. Runs furnish a slightly sparser supply of slightly larger insects and some crustaceans. Pools provide crayfish, baitfish, leeches, and sculpins as the primary sources of food. The increasing size of the prey is part of the reason that trout move through a simple progression as they grow larger, establishing successive territories first in riffles, then runs, and finally pools.

When a trout takes up residence in one of the best lies in a pool, it is usually of a size to take advantage of the larger food offered there. It is also usually large enough to swat smaller trout out of its way.

The bottom of a pool is usually poor soil for aquatic insects. But trout in a pool are the recipients of hatches that occur in the riffle or run upstream from the pool. The drift at the head of a pool can be extremely rich. Hatches are also excellent at times on tailouts. If the hatch is heavy, the largest trout in a pool will sometimes back down with the current to hold lazily and pick insects above the shallows.

When selecting flies to match the foods of pools, it's best to match the biggest bites if you want to take the largest trout. You want to use something with sufficient size to stimulate the urge to feed in a trout that might have just eaten, and is not interested in moving far for the next meal unless it's a big one.

Trout are not always active in pools. They tend instead to engulf a large meal, then spend a few hours to a few days digesting

Sculpin.

it. The larger the trout, the less often it feeds, assuming it gets the kind of large meal it likes.

Temperature and Oxygen

If there's a bad place for a trout to be in a stream when temperatures get high and oxygen levels get low, it's in a pool. The water is still, or nearly so, and there is little exchange to freshen it. That doesn't necessarily mean trout will move out of it; depth in itself is some shield from heat in a pool that is several feet deep.

If conditions approach distressing, trout in pools will slow down and nearly cease to function. It's a good place to do it, because there is little current to fight, and fish can put things on hold without getting pushed out of their holding lies.

When conditions are severe, trout will move out of pools and seek riffles and even rapids, hanging in pockets surrounded by white water where they would not normally be found. When temperatures are high and oxygen low, there are better places to fish than pools.

The exceptions to the above are pools that benefit from underwater springs. These are rare, especially in freestone streams, but if you find one you will find a hot spot. A cool sidestream freshet creates the same conditions, cooling the main body of the pool. It is well to notice the arrival of feeder creeks along the course of a stream; when conditions get bad in the heat of summer, you can try the pools immediately downstream. If the water of the feeder is cool enough, its freshening effect might continue for several hundred feet.

TYPES OF POOLS

There are different kinds of pools, defined largely by the way a stream creates them.

Classic pools are places where the river simply pauses to rest. They are wide, deep, and dark; the water is nearly as slow as a farm pond. Classic pools have the simple anatomy already described: head, body, and tailout.

Large classic pools are relatively rare on most rivers, though it might seem they are common until we close our eyes and ransack our minds to think of where we've seen them. There are none on such famous rivers as the Deschutes and the upper Madison. But they are important features on rivers like the Big Hole, and many famous Catskill rivers have the traditional trout-stream structure of riffle to run to classic pool, then back to riffle and run again.

Classic pools are much more common on smaller streams. Chances are your home water has them, and chances are you fish their tailouts sometimes, their bodies almost never, and their heads almost always. The order should be the opposite, since the largest trout in a pool holds in its tailout sometimes, its body almost always, and its head almost never.

Bend pools are what we think about when we think about pools. They are found where the river takes a change in course. The current sweeps around the outside of the curve, eroding it away, digging it deeper. The flow of a bend pool is slow, but it

Typical pool in a large western river.

seldom loses its definition as a current. In some ways bend pools border on being runs. But they are separated from runs by the depths they achieve, six to ten or more feet, with shallower water leading in and out of them.

Most bend pools are broad and sweeping, with shallow gravel bars on the inside of the turn and a deep cut on the outside. Almost all trout waters have some bend pools, but they are most common in large streams and in trout rivers. Meadow streams, with their meandering courses cut through level river bottoms, have cut-bank bend pools sprinkled at almost regular intervals.

Cliff pools are bend pools where the water arrives at a fairly abrupt angle against an immovable object: a giant boulder, a cliff, or a solid bank that the water has worked an indent into. The flow stacks up before making its turn. The result is a deep undercut eroded at the turn, forming a short deep pool.

Ledge-rock pools form wherever the stream has worked its way to solid rock, then eroded a deep channel down it. These pools tend to be abruptly deep, very narrow, and banked in tightly on both sides. They are features of a fairly steep geography and are found toward the upper end of a stream system, where it still dwells in the foothills or the mountains.

Plunge pools are sometimes strung like pearls on a necklace down the course of mountain streams with steep gradients. They are formed by water tumbling over obstructions, one after another, eroding pockets below. The water might drop from a miniature waterfall, or it might plunge down from several feet. The pool itself might be brief and frothed, just a few feet long. Or it might be wide and spreading and deep.

In my experience, plunge pools that form holding lies slightly larger than those typical for the stream also produce fish slightly larger than those average for the stream. Larger plunge pools that are formed below tall waterfalls, on the other hand, always look better but produce less, at least for me.

Plunge pools also form below waterfalls in low-gradient streams, farther down the system. These are always perfect places to take pictures of folks fishing, but they are rarely any more productive than the riffles and runs and pools up and down the rest of the stream. Rivers that have upstream spawning migrations, however, gather frustrated fish in waterfall pools. They

Plunge pool formed by a waterfall in a small mountain stream.

can be excellent places to fish if you don't mind fishing over thwarted trout.

Eddy pools are common on most rivers. They are places where a strong current swings out from the bank. The water along the side of the main current shifts into the space next to the abandoned bank. It finds a vacuum there and noses back upstream to see where it's been. When it goes full circle and joins the main current to go downstream again, it has left an eddy in its wake.

The resulting backwater has a permanent circular current. It forms a gentle place for trout to hold, with depth and therefore excellent protection from predation. As a bonus to trout, an eddy is a trap for all the debris and all the drift that comes down the current. Trout can hold anywhere in it, feeding quietly on aquatic insects and terrestrials and anything else caught on the conveyor that goes round and round. Because eddy trout are picky and eddy currents are conflicting and confusing, they are extremely difficult to fish.

HOLDING LIES IN POOLS

The holding lies in a pool are analogous to the parts of the pool: the head, body, and tailout. Any obstructions that slow the current in the moving parts of the pool or that offer extra shelter in the depths of the pool will also form excellent lies.

The Head of a Pool

The head of a pool is usually a current tongue rushing in from a riffle or run above. It is a prime place for trout to hold: the sudden deepening of the pool slows the water and provides shelter from the current; depth, and the frothed current of the current tongue, give protection from predators; the current delivers feed produced in the water upstream. Trout lies at the head of a pool are generally in the slight eddies formed off to the sides of the entering current, or else down on the bottom, directly beneath the current. This water is very similar to the corners of riffles and runs, and holds trout for the same reasons: it's the best place in which to hide and from which to spear out to take advantage of food that a rich current trots by.

Often a pool is formed by a shelf or drop-off at the head, followed by water that is of uniform depth down to the tailout. When this is true, the best holding water in the pool is located in the first few feet, right under the entering current tongue, since the most shelter, protection, and feed are all located right there. The rest of the pool, with its even depth, will hold trout. But the prime lie will be at the head of the pool.

The Body of a Pool

In a typical pool the water depth slopes off downstream from the head. The body of a pool thus formed might not always hold the greatest concentration of trout, but it is likely to hold the largest trout. They lurk in the quiet depths, waiting for a chance at something worth eating, letting trout that are still gaining their growth stay up at the head of the pool to argue over tidbits that arrive on the drift.

The body of a plunge pool in a small mountain creek usually holds one dominant trout. Others might rush your fly in peripheral waters; the largest trout will usually occupy the lie that offers it the first and best shot at whatever food the pool brings. That is why it is often best to stalk these tiny pools carefully and present your first cast to the most likely holding water rather than fish your way up through them. If you fish poor water first you are likely to hook a small fish first. Its antics will spoil the pool before you can show your fly to the bully of it.

The body of a medium-sized pool might hold several fish nearly equal in size. Sometimes it holds a dominant fish, one that has established such a favorable territory that it has outgrown its competitors by what amounts to lots of heft if you ever get a chance to hold it in your hand.

A pool in a large western river might be the size of a farm pond, and it might hold many large trout. Each fish will usually have its own territory when resting. But recall that the urge toward territoriality is relaxed as the water approaches stillness. These trout are hunters. They spend most of their time in torpor, or near it, digesting the last meal. When it is time to hunt they forage throughout the pool, sticking to the protection of its depths in daytime but moving up into the shallows along the edges, or onto the tailout, at dawn and dusk.

The Tailout of a Pool

The tailout delivers a pool to whatever is below it. Some tailouts lift and then plunge into cascades so swiftly that they are not fishable. But most lift gently, thinning and fanning out until they ease over into the run or riffle below. Tailouts have some of the aspects of riffles, with a bottom of fairly uniform gravel that is rich in insect life. But the surface lacks the chop of a riffle. The result can be fast water that is slick on top, a combination that leads to some tough fishing.

Trout usually do not hold on a brisk tailout unless some sort of insect or other activity entices them there. The water lacks sufficient shelter from currents, and protection from predators, to make these tailouts anything but feeding lies. But they can be rich in aquatic insects, and trout are often drawn there to feed.

Some slow tailouts have all of the aspects of rich flats. Their thinness promotes photosynthetic growth, and they have prolific hatches. Their gentle currents do not even require shelter. But the skinny water offers little protection from bird predation. I have encountered lots of trout holding in gentle tailouts, usually right at the lip. These trout are seldom large, although there have been exceptions. They are invariably wary, completing the analogy to flats, where trout flee at the faintest sign of passing substance or shadow.

Shallow tailouts are excellent places for sculpins, baitfish, and crayfish to forage. They usually become active in the morning or at evening, when light is low. The same low light prompts large trout to leave the sanctuary of the body of the pool, to come out to forage on the foragers. That is why you are liable to take small fish at the lower lip of a pool during the day, but often set the hook into something that has trouble keeping its dorsal fin submerged in the thin water of a tailout at dawn and dusk.

Obstructions in Pools

The head, body, and tailout of a pool are all obvious lies for trout at one time or another. But within these parts of a pool, tip-offs to specific holding lies are the same as they are in other parts of the stream. Any boulder or log or shelving area in the head area of the pool will interrupt the fast inflow of water and will allow trout to hold in shelter from the current.

Large boulders in the head, body, or tailout of a pool are natural havens for all sorts of crayfish and baitfish, and offer maximum shelter to trout at the same time they feed them. Logs and root wads are commonly caught in the slow water of pools, especially along the edges of bend pools. These offer special comfort to the largest fish. They are among the toughest places to fish, which is why they hold the largest fish. In a stream with heavy fishing pressure, any hindrance to the angler is bound to be considered shelter by the trout, since fishing pressure becomes one of the major shaping forces in the activity of the fish: We become the main predators.

STRATEGIES FOR FISHING POOLS

When thinking of tactics for pools, it is best to consider the anatomy of the pool and dissect it into head, body, and tailout, rather than into the three layers dealt with in riffles and runs: the bottom, mid-depths, and top.

The head of a pool, where the water enters with a strong flow from the riffle or run above, is best fished with an extension of the tactics you were using when you arrived there. The water takes on the characteristics of whatever forms it; if it's a riffle, fish it as a riffle; if it's a run, fish it as a run.

The tailout has most of the characteristics of a riffle and should be fished with the tactics described for that type of water. But it can also be slick on top, like a flat, making it necessary to fish it with finer tactics. If trout feed actively, you are often forced to match the natural insect with a dressing that is at least a fairly close representation in order to take trout from tailouts.

Tackle for Fishing Pools

The principle of matching the rod to the river makes as much sense when discussing pools as it does when discussing riffles and runs. You will encounter a stream's pools as you come to them, fishing all the water. If the rod suits the size of the stream, you should be able to fish its pools without problems. If you are undergunned for the rest of the river it will show up most when you bump into a pool.

Most of us choose tackle as light as we dare when fishing for trout. That is a large part of the reason big pools are not fished a lot: we aren't often armed to fish them, so we skip around them.

If you were to choose gear to fish just the pools along the course of a stream, you might choose it one size heavier than normal. A mid-sized trout stream that calls for a long number-six rod to fish its riffles and runs might be fished a bit better with a rod that tosses number-seven lines. But in this age of graphite rods, most six-weight rods cast seven-weight lines without problems. Carry an extra spool with a line that is a size heavier than that specified for your rod and you're in business to fish pools. In fact, the heavier line has the advantage of slowing the rod down a bit, which can make it a better choice for lobbing some of the bombs that fish best in pools.

The largest trout in any stream will hold in its deep pools. *(photo by Tony Robnett)*

Fortunately, the size of a bomb is relative. A bomb in a tiny creek is a #10 fly. In a mid-sized trout stream, it might be a #6 or #8. You can fish these bombs with the normal run of gear you would use for the size stream you happen to be on.

When we think of pools, we think of big water in big rivers. Bombs in such water are small at size two, and often splash down tied on 2/0 hooks. If you are going to propel such things, your tackle must be chosen to accomplish the job.

Special gear for big pools, then, should be big gear. The rod should be nine to nine and a half feet long. The line it lofts should be at least an eight-weight, but for the heaviest flies a nine- or even ten-weight works better. This kind of equipment is not particularly versatile; you don't want to be stuck with it in a situation where you want to make a delicate presentation with a

#24 gnat. But you also don't want to be stuck with gnat-sized equipment when you want to pitch pool-sized flies.

On a recent two-week trip to Montana I made the mistake of taking a light but fast-action six-weight rod as my *heavy*. It was perfect for fishing drys, wets, and all but the largest and heaviest nymphs. But I pelted myself with so many big weighted flies, failed to reach the best water so often, and caught so few trout over a pound, that I wound up the trip frustrated as hell.

Since that trip I've discovered that my summer steelhead rod, a nine-foot reserve power graphite that normally fishes a double-taper six line, slows down and makes a good lobbing rod when overloaded with a number-eight weight-forward line. It's a fact you should keep in mind. You might already own the perfect big rod, if only you give it a chance with the right line. But if I did this kind of fishing more often, I would have a rod that cast a number-nine line without compromise.

In the last chapter, when considering tackle for fishing in runs, I advised the addition of a spare reel spool carrying a wet-tip line in a fast but not super-fast sink rate. For pools, you want to go at least one step deeper. There are two ways you can do it. The first is by carrying a fast-sinking wet-head line with the first thirty feet designed to sink. The second is with a ten-foot wet-tip line that is super-fast-sinking.

The full-sinking head has two advantages: it is a little easier to cast, and it all sinks. It tends to keep the fly down on the bottom with a level retrieve, rather than climbing upward toward the floating part of the line. The super-fast wet-tip also has two advantages: it plummets quickly, and it leaves you more floating line to control the drift and to watch for indications of a strike.

I prefer the wet-head, since I prefer whatever leaves an element of grace in my casting, and since I expect my hits in pools to be reported without subtlety. That is my prejudice. You should try both and see what works best for you. Whichever it is, keep it firmly seated in your mind that a slow rod works best when you are casting heavy lines and weighted flies. A fast rod will teach you to flinch every time you lean into a forward cast.

When you decide to specialize in the largest pools, with the largest trout in mind, you might choose a shooting-head system. This consists of a thirty-foot casting line looped to one hundred feet of running line, either monofilament or a two-weight level floating fly line. The shooting system works best if you attach the heads with loops. Then you can carry a series of them — slow-sinking, fast-sinking, and super-fast — to cover all kinds of pools. You can remove one and replace it with another in just a minute or so. If you have to reel up and switch spools and restring your line through the guides every time you want to fish a different depth, you're not likely to do it, not if you are at all like me. I don't think I'm lazy, but I am modestly impatient. I'll bet you are, too.

This shooting-head system is the same one discussed in the chapter on runs, for fishing big western rivers. It is useful on all big water, and on lakes, too. Most of the time when you fish water that calls for such gear you'll be using a boat for transportation. It's more than just handy to have something big to reach for when you come upon big water: big water is big-fish water, and you want to be properly armed to fish it.

Whatever kind of sinking system you use, keep the leader short — three or four feet — and it will not buoy the fly back up after the line has taken it down.

Fishing the Head of a Pool

The head of a pool is something of a funnel for food that arrives from above. The flies, tackle, and tactics chosen to fish it should be dependent on what kind of water enters the pool, not on the form of the pool itself. If the head of the run taps the foot of a riffle, it gives you a clue to the size of the insects that will be delivered down the currents. Choose the same kinds of flies that were used to explore riffled water and you won't go far wrong. Nymphs such as the Zug Bug and Gold-Ribbed Hare's Ear, in sizes ten and twelve, slightly weighted, resemble a lot of the nymphs and larvae that a pool trout sees getting washed down to it every day.

Trout will also move for wets at the heads of pools that originate in the ends of riffles: lots of insects arrive to them in the drift. The same flies and the same presentations that worked in the riffle above will continue to work as you fish your way out of the riffle and down into the head of the run.

If the water at the head of a pool is shallow enough, usually not more than four or five feet, trout will often move to the surface for dry flies. The current tongue itself, and the eddied water to both sides of it, are excellent places to deliver a dry. It should be larger than the normal fly you would use on a riffle, because the trout must be tempted into rising farther to take it.

If the water feeding into the head of the pool is a run, large nymphs fished deep are usually the best bet. Cast them into the water that forms the current tongue, a few feet above the start of the pool, so that they have time to sink before they reach the prime lies downstream. When they have reached the end of their natural drift, coax them through the side eddies. If the current tongue is narrow enough, and your rod long enough, try to probe the eddy on the far side of the current. But this will only be possible on small streams. On larger water you will have to find a way to cross over in order to fish both sides of the current that enters a pool.

The mid-depths and surface at the head of a pool fed by a run can be productive at times, but only when some sort of insect activity has the attention of trout focused upward. This is not an uncommon condition; whenever there is a hatch in the run above, a high percentage of the insects are delivered to the pool below. That is the major reason the head of the pool is such a favored holding lie.

Fishing dry at the head of a pool, when the water is more than five or six feet deep, should be tied to some sort of visible feeding activity. If you see trout rising, try to determine what they are taking. Match it as nearly as you can, and present the imitation in a natural manner. If fish are not actively feeding, it is not out of line to try to drum them up with an Elk Hair Caddis or Royal Wulff. But don't expect to do wonderfully all of the time. If you don't catch anything, and you are a dry fly purist, simply change the water type you are fishing. If you can't get fish to rise at the head of the pool, move on up to the riffle or run above it.

Fishing the Body of a Pool

There are three variables to work with when fishing the body of a pool: fly pattern, retrieve, and depth.

Fly patterns for the depths of pools should be large, large being anything from a #6 tied on a long-shank hook, up to a #2/0. In some places there is a movement to the use of outsize flies constructed to imitate hatchery trout, baby muskrats, and other things that might make you think it best to keep your toes out of water that contains trout that could eat them.

I fished the Metolius River one dawn with John Judy, author of the finely honed little book *The Metolius.* John is an expert on the big Dolly Varden trout known to hold in his home river.

We arrived at his favorite Dolly hole at daylight but were surprised to find three people already fishing it. Paul Peterson, another Dolly expert and also the owner of a store and fly shop on the river, was guiding two clients in quest of a large trout. There was only one place from which a fly could be fished properly, so John and I sat under a ponderosa and waited a chance to take a turn. We watched Paul's clients fish for half an hour.

The hole was a strange one, a sharp drop into a pool at the end of a fast five-foot-deep run. The pool itself was about seventy feet downstream from the nearest place you could wade into the edge of the run far enough to cast. The procedure for fishing the hole became clear to me as I watched Paul's first client fish. He wound up like a baseball pitcher, flung a huge fly back over his shoulder to load the line and cock the rod, then lobbed it forward about forty feet, straight out into the run, where it landed with a splat. The *fly* was about the size and weight of a dead rabbit.

As soon as the fly landed, mends were tossed into the line and slack fed out, so the giant fly drifted freely down the run, toward the hole. A high-density line tugged it deep. When the fly passed over the end of the run and fell into the head of the hole, the rod was lifted, the line drawn tight, and the fly coaxed around with a teasing swing.

To complicate matters, the fly swam right at a giant log lodged lengthwise at the head of the pool. It was obvious that any big fish in the pool would be hunkered under that log. The idea was to retrieve the fly so it swam toward the log, then pull it free at the last second so that it didn't try to swim under the log and get snagged.

After each of his clients had tried this for half an hour, Paul himself stepped in and cast for another twenty minutes, using the same technique. He finally turned the pool over to John Judy. John tried a special fly, tied out of a chunk of rabbit hide folded over and sewn together, with a tandem of 2/0 hooks snelled in the fold. I have the fly sitting on my desk, next to a ruler, as I write: it's over seven inches long and fat as a frightened cat's tail. John lobbed and retrieved this fly for fifteen minutes, but it failed to move a fish.

Finally it was my turn. The light rod I carried would not have propelled one of those flies five feet. Paul loaned me his. But he changed flies before he did. He tied on a tarpon fly. I don't know that the pattern has a name. It imitates a hatchery trout, at least on the Metolius River. It is tied on a 3/0 saltwater hook. The underwing is white bucktail, the upper wing blue FisHair. There are stringers of tinsel along the entire length, and a white head the size of a pencil end. I have this fly on my desk, too, next to the ruler. It is nine and a half inches long. If I caught it on one of my small mountain creeks, I could keep it and fry it next to the stream for dinner.

I insisted on backcasting this monster in order to feel I was fly fishing rather than pitching at a baseball game. My first cast nearly decapitated some squirrels in the ponderosa woods behind me but got the fly out forty feet into the run in front of me. I frantically stripped off line and tossed it into the drift of the fly. When Paul, calling down directions from high on the bank behind me, told me the time was right, I stopped the line, lifted the rod, and teased the fly into its swimming arc toward the log.

The fly felt heavy. I said to Paul over my shoulder, "This thing is so big it feels like you have a fish on when it comes around in the current." I turned back to the fly, stripped in more line, and tried to give it a couple more teasing tugs. But the thing kept getting heavier and heavier.

The rod bent lower and lower. When its tip was down near the water I reared back on it, as if to ask it a question: "What the hell's going on out there?"

The answer was a strong tug back.

For a minute the fish or the fly or whatever it was felt loggy. Then it took off down toward the bottom of the hole, under that log. I brutalized it out of there, forced it up into the run, and held on while it tired itself out thrashing around in the fast water.

The fish did not put up a brilliant fight. A brown or rainbow in the same kind of heavy water would likely have torn me up. But the Dolly wasted its strength on the current, then came out to the edge of it and over my hand without much struggle. I hefted it out of the water for some photos, then slipped out the 3/0 hook and slid the fish back toward its home in the hole. It needed to grow; it was a fairly small one, only six pounds.

I looked at the fly, shook my head at the size of it, and handed the rod back to Paul. "I'd be a damned fool to take another cast," I told him.

When fishing the body of a pool, your fly should be selected based on two things: the size of the fish you hope to catch, and the size of the bites you think that fish most commonly eats. That Dolly on the Metolius was a few hundred yards downstream from the outlet of a fish hatchery. What it ate came flopping down the chute once a week.

All big trout are rapacious, though not quite so fierce as Dolly Vardens. They don't all feed on hatchery trout or baby muskrats, but they all like big bites.

If the fish you hope for weighs two to four pounds, then you could expect it to feed most often on sculpins, crayfish, and small fish. Though it undoubtedly likes them larger when it can capture them, most of its meals will be around two to three inches long. These are imitated well on hook sizes two and four, long shank. You can go a lot bigger, but the guides I have talked to in Montana feel that flies tied on #2 hooks will interest the largest fish there, that they are reasonably easy to cast, and that larger flies increase the difficulty of casting without increasing the size of the catch.

The most popular flies for big trout are sculpin imitations such as Muddlers and Spuddlers, Woolly Buggers in black and olive, streamers such as the Spruce, and big ugly nymphs like the Bitch Creek or Yuk Bug. There are lots of other flies that work as well. Zonkers are favorites in lots of areas. Strip Leeches work well for large trout. My personal favorite is the Black Marabou Muddler, simply because the first time I used one, it produced well for me, and I now reach for it whenever I expect to catch anything, which means it gets fished in all the lucrative situations. Most of the time I tie it on smaller hooks, #6 and #8. For larger pools, where I expect larger trout, I use it as large as #2.

There are two theories on whether flies for pools should be

Typical flies for fishing pools.

weighted or unweighted. The first theory is that the line should be used to get the fly down, and the fly itself should be left unweighted so it moves more naturally in the water. The second theory says the fly should be heavily weighted so it gets down and bumps the very bottom no matter what kind of line is used. Everybody must choose what suits best. Some people don't like to cast fast-sinking lines, preferring to cast heavily weighted flies. Others don't like to cast weighted flies, preferring to cast dense lines.

My own practice treads middle ground. I weight my large flies moderately, with about ten to fifteen turns of lead wire the diameter of the hook shank. This is enough weight to get them under the surface quickly. They work well when cast tight to banks, from a boat, along the edge water of long runs. An unweighted fly in this situation might not sink at all; it will catch few fish when retrieved so shallow it leaves a wake.

A fly weighted this way, modestly by western standards, gets down fast when fished with a sinking line. But it still has some life, some movement of its own, when fished on the bottom. If the fly were weighted like a stone, it might also fish like a stone.

Once you've chosen your fly pattern, retrieve is the second consideration. There are essentially three speeds of retrieve: fast, medium, and none. The first is often the best, because it imitates the movement of a lot of the trout foods that big fish eat. And it imitates them trying to escape, which is what trout expect things to do when they prepare to eat them.

A medium-speed stripping retrieve is also excellent because it represents the stop-and-go movement with which most natural foods swim most of the time.

No retrieve at all works only where there is enough current to give the fly some action. If the pool has a fair flow, it sometimes works best to cast the fly out, let it get right down to the bottom, then let it tumble along at the request of the current. This is the way a lot of food is delivered to trout, and though there is no indication that they feed much on critters that are already dead, chances are the current will give your fly enough movement to make it look alive.

One retrieve works best at one time; the next time it fails to move fish at all and another retrieve works best. You've got to experiment until you find the one that fish want. Alternate retrieves on successive casts. Sometimes you can try all three retrieves on the same cast: let the fly sink to the bottom and dead-drift a ways, then pick it up and tease it around the low end of its arc on a medium-speed retrieve, and finally bring it back to you with fast strips that swim it through the water at a trot.

The final factor is depth. The body of a pool has no mid-depths and no surface. Forget them. If fish are out cruising, they will not be doing it in the middle of deep water. They will move to the head, the tailout, or the edges of the pool, where the water is shallow and stream life is richer. For purposes of reading water, consider all but the bottom of the body of a pool to be a wasteland. If you fish anywhere but near the bottom, you will largely waste your time.

It is not always easy to accomplish getting your fly right to the bottom of a deep pool. It can be damned hard. You can think you are doing it while missing by several feet. I'm not good at it myself. I haven't set up lunker-hunting as much of a goal in life. But if you want big fish, then think *bottom* unless fish are moving.

It is best to take up a casting position at the side of the pool, if the shape of the pool allows it, where you can quarter your casts slightly upstream. Let the fly and line sink, and make your retrieve as the fly swings slightly downstream below you. This gives you the best control. But the pool often dictates the way you can fish it.

If you must fish from the head of the pool, and it has much current, you will need a faster-sinking line, since the current will serve to buoy the line and fly upward. If you are forced to fish from the tail of the pool, your line might be a slower sinker because the current coming toward you will let the line and fly sink more swiftly. In this case you will want to speed up your

Fishing the body of a large pool from its head.

retrieve; you have to activate the fly in relation to the current, not in relation to the bottom.

If there is little or no current in the pool, you can fish it from any direction and achieve the same result. What you want to attain is a fly that swims within a foot of the bottom. You should be feeling it touch now and then, or you're not fishing deep enough. Expect to lose an occasional fly if you are fishing a large pool right.

Remember that it's dark down there. The trout you are after might not see the fly unless it comes very near. Don't just take a cast or two and assume you've covered the pool. Set up a disciplined pattern that covers all of the deep water. If you *know* there are big fish down there, set up a pattern that covers all of the water twice, or three times. When you are after one big fish rather than a bunch of little ones, all of the patience you can gather will be needed somewhere along the line. It doesn't happen very often that you catch a six-pound trout on the first cast.

The body of a pool is a bit like a pond or a lake. There are the three variables — fly pattern, speed of retrieve, and depth fished — that you must experiment with until you find the right combination. The fly pattern should be one you've developed confidence in. But switch if you've been persistent and your favorite fly hasn't produced. The depth should be near the bottom, but experiment until you've found the right line, and the right amount of sinking time, to get your fly down there and fish it right. The right retrieve is generally about three times as fast as most people think would frighten a fastidious trout. But there are times when a dead slow retrieve works best. It never hurts to try something different every few casts, just by way of testing the waters.

Fishing the Tailout of a Pool

The tailout of a pool is less complicated than its head or body. It should be fished as you would fish a riffle or run, keying your fly selection, tackle, and tactics to the hatch that draws fish into active feeding there. Most of the time the insects will be relatively small. Often you will be forced to match the hatch, since the surface of a tailout tends to be smooth.

The three-layered approach to fishing — the bottom, mid-depths, and top – is important again when tackling tailouts. Trout often feed on drift that is close to the bottom. They also feed regularly on aquatic insects in the vital transition from bottom to top, in the mid-depths zone. When the greatest concentration of food is on the surface, trout will hang high in the water and feed willingly on the top.

Fishing nymphs along the bottom of a tailout calls for upstream tactics, similar to those used in a riffle, with weighted flies, a long leader, and a dry line. A strike indicator placed about twice the depth of the water above the fly will increase the number of takes you detect.

Probing the mid-depths of a tailout with a wet fly can be one of the most effective tactics available, one that is rarely used today. I use the downstream wet fly swing almost by choice when fish feed visibly in the thin water of tailouts. Even if I see adult insects on the water, my success is usually better in these situations when I select a wet fly the color and size of the natural and present it just under the surface. This works especially well on broad tailouts, where it is difficult to wade into position for dry-fly presentations.

Fishing dry flies on tailouts works well if you can wade into a good position. But there are things that make it unlikely. First, the water accelerates on the lip of the tailout; casting from downstream subjects the fly to drag after just a few inches of float. Second, it is difficult to approach from upstream, since that is the deep part of the pool and it's difficult to cast well while treading water. There are tailouts where you can wade laterally and fish with casts straight across stream. But they are not as common as one would like.

The difficulty getting into position for a dry-fly presentation is the major reason I have most of my success on tailouts with wet flies. I can cast long, from a position at the outside edge of the tailout, and swim the fly across the lip, where the trout feed. Drag would kill any hope for success with a dry fly. With the wet, drag keeps the fly swimming across, looking like an emerging insect on its way to the surface. But it mustn't race; if a wet fly gets going too fast, trout consult their books on aquatic entomology, find nothing that moves that way, and ignore it.

When large trout come out to forage in the tailout, usually at dawn or dusk, the same tactic works well, but with a lot larger fly. The same Muddlers and Woolly Buggers and Marabous that worked in the body of the pool will work in the tailout when large fish feed there. Fish them on lines that keep them just under the surface. In the shallow water at the tail of a pool you don't have to worry about getting your fly down to the bottom. Trout will see it at any level.

If a large trout is actively hunting and it spots your large fly, it will most often wallop it.

8

The Challenge of Fishing Flats

Tilt a flat a bit and you wouldn't have one. Flats are shallow water, from one to four feet deep, with gentle gradients that produce slow flows and a smooth surface. If a flat were steeper it would flow faster, no vegetation could take root, and the bottom would be a collection of coarser material: cobble and rock. The surface would reflect the roughness of the bottom and you would have a riffle or run, depending on its depth.

STRUCTURE OF A FLAT

A flat is a reach of stream where the water slows, as it does in a pool. But instead of nearly stopping, it retains its defined current; instead of deepening, it spreads out, with an almost even depth from side to side. Because the water is slow, the finest material is allowed to settle to the bottom.

Many flats have bottoms of fine cobble and pebbles. Most have at least some sediment and sand mixed in with the stones. This has two results: first, the smooth bottom is responsible for a glassy surface; second, the bottom makes fine soil for rooted aquatic vegetation.

The water in a flat is shallow. Sunlight strikes through and photosynthetic growth is at least as rich as it is in a riffle. But the current of a flat is gentle. In a riffle, vegetation is constantly scoured out; it doesn't get a chance to get a grip on the bottom. In flats, weed beds are so common that they are part of the definition of the water type. Productive flats are almost always set apart from unproductive flats by the growth of rooted vegetation or attached algae. Such growth indicates current speeds that are extremely suitable to trout, the growth itself offers a richness of insect life, and it also offers protection from predators in water that would otherwise be relatively barren of trout.

The Railroad Ranch section of The Henry's Fork of the Snake River, in Idaho, is the ultimate flat. It has two major sources, one a spring creek, the other controlled by water released from Island Park Reservoir. Its flows are steady, and the long broad flats are not subject to scour. The entire bottom is bearded with a growth of weeds that grow longer as the season gets older.

The ranch reach is about three miles long. In the upper mile most of the river is about one hundred yards wide and can be waded across with some caution. It averages three feet deep, but there are some surprise trenches a foot or two deeper. The current is steady, firm, but easily waded against. In the middle mile or so of the reach, the river spreads out farther, deepens in places so that wading requires extreme caution, and the current slows to almost nil. Farther down, there is a brief stretch of rapids, then another half mile of flat before the river flows under the highway and out of the ranch section.

The water is spring-creek clear. The great weed beds are hot-beds of insect growth. Hatches are heavy, sometimes so heavy that you want to wade to shore in disgust because it seems the chance a trout might select your artificial among hundreds of naturals would be remote. Sometimes it is remote. Sometimes it is better to mismatch the hatch in hopes a trout will take your fly because it is *different*, than it is to match the hatch.

Rainbow trout work in pods across The Henry's Fork flats. They move slowly upstream, feeding as they go on whatever insect is coming off at the moment. After a hundred feet or so,

which might take fifteen minutes or two hours, they seem to drop out of sight for a few minutes, then materialize again, rising at the lower end of their favored water to begin working up once more.

Fishermen work on the pods, spreading themselves out. Through the compression of a telephoto lens it can be made to look like they are so close that their backcasts would tangle in the air. But they are a comfortable distance apart, and each has his own pod of trout to work over. It is the only place in the world that I have fished in what I would normally call a crowd without feeling crowded. The single time I saw a problem was when a guide in a high-prowed drift boat fished a client down through the ranch flats during a Green Drake hatch.

The boat was unnecessary. The guide waded at the bow and slowly pushed the boat downstream while his client stood in the boat and beat the water. The client caught no fish; he had no chance of catching any fish the way he went about it. The guide was probably trying to hurry him down to the riffles.

Apparently the client knew nothing of stream etiquette, or he would have jumped overboard, splashed to shore, and run off

through the bordering fields in shame. The guide carried out his paid mission with his head tilted slightly downward, his cowboy hat hiding his eyes. Anglers working their pods moved out of the way of the boat with curious backward glances, then closed in behind it and waited for the fish to begin working again. It didn't take long. Nobody said anything, which was to everyone's credit.

We tend to associate flats with spring creeks. They have more flats than freestone streams simply because they are not subject to scour from winter spate and spring runoff. But flats are a result of a stream's gradient as well as its source. Most freestone streams have occasional reaches that are just as flat, and just as difficult to fish, as spring creek flats. My friends and I fish the Deschutes River and the Willamette River in Oregon several times each year. Our favorite drifts on each river have reaches that we nickname The Henry's Fork.

The Henry's Fork of the Deschutes is two hundred yards of side current. It is fifty yards wide, three to four feet deep in toward shore, and too deep to wade twenty feet out from it. The flat has a sandy bottom with lots of trailing weed beds. It has a strong but even current and a flat surface. Trout rise consistently to hatches,

**Richard Bunse fishing the Railroad Ranch flats on The Henry's Fork of the
Snake River.**

and the tactics that take them are the same that we use on spring
creek flats. It is not legal to fish from a boat on the Deschutes; the
trout that rise out of reach on this flat are always at least twice
the size of the fourteen- to sixteen-inchers we catch in the part of
it that we are able to wade.

The Henry's Fork of the Willamette is at the tailout of a pool
that is a quarter-mile long, more than a hundred yards wide. The
water rises up to between four and five feet deep, maintaining
this depth for the last hundred yards of the pool. It has a rocky
bottom and little attached vegetation. Its current is easy and its
surface is smooth.

Fish constantly rise on this flat tailout, feeding selectively on
tiny mayflies, caddisflies, and stoneflies. The water is too deep to

wade safely. We drift down it in boats, anchor, fish a stretch, then raise the anchor and lower the boat a few feet down the current before dropping the anchor again. Fish rise right at the end of the oars, but it can be exceedingly difficult to determine what stage of what insect they are taking and to find a fly that imitates it successfully.

I find the fishing easier to solve on the real Henry's Fork than I do on The Henry's Fork of the Willamette.

Freestone streams have many unproductive rocky flats that border on riffles. These are generally empty water, and you should learn to recognize them so you don't spend a lot of time fishing them. They are usually long and broad, a foot or at most two feet deep, with bottoms of such uniform cobble that there are very few places for fish to shelter. The surface of such a flat might be smooth, or it might have a slight chop; it depends on its speed. Whichever it is, it will be unfeatured, and water without features, as I've noted before, is usually water without trout.

These kinds of flats are either too fast to allow the growth of aquatic vegetation or they suffer scour during winter storms and spring runoff. They do have excellent populations of aquatic insects, and trout might move up into them to feed if a hatch is heavy. For the most part, though, trout avoid such flats because they have to fight the current and risk predation, which makes such water uneconomical places to be.

Riffled flats are prime whitefish water, and populations of the two kinds of fish seldom overlap.

THE NEEDS OF TROUT

Flats meet the needs of trout, or fail to meet them, in predictable ways.

Shelter from Currents

The need for shelter from currents is met easily, for the currents are gentle and little protection is needed from them. The extensive weed beds that typify flats create a pattern of channels and eddies and still pockets that give trout lots of places to shelter. Most trout on flats find their comfort in weed-bed cover.

There are a few features on most flats: boulders, trenches, stranded logs, and anything else that finds itself lodged in a current too subtle to wash it away. All of these break the current and form protective lies. Trout tend to hold in them when not feeding. When a hatch happens, there might be as many insects around these kinds of cover as there are elsewhere, so trout tend to remain on their lies unless the lies fail to feed them.

Protection from Predators

Protection from predators is the smallest common denominator on flats. The water is shallow, as clear as trout-stream water gets, and smooth on top. There is little to impede the sight or hinder the attack of an osprey from overhead. But the same weeds and occasional obstructions that provide shelter from minimal currents also provide protection from predators when fish are resting.

When trout feed on flats, they must move out into the open, exposing themselves. As mentioned in the first chapter, trout are greedy and willing to risk danger, even to the extent of a tithe of their number, in order to feed when a food form is abundant and available. On flats during the trout season, some sort of insect usually makes itself available at one time or another during the course of a day, and trout are drawn out of their hides. When they expose themselves on flats, trout are as wary as trout get.

Trout Foods on Flats

The need for food is met on a flat by the great abundance of insects and crustaceans that live in the weed beds. The reason was pointed out by the ever-observant Charlie Brooks: *vertical use*. Insects are not confined to the first few inches of the substrate, where they find niches in the gravel bottom. Instead, they have use of the entire water column, wherever there are weeds. The result can be astonishing numbers of aquatic insects.

Caddis of the case-making types are abundant on some flats. A few stonefly species, usually the smaller varieties, also do well in the gentle flows of flats. But the most abundant and important aquatic insects are the mayflies. In general, the smallest species have adapted to the weed beds. Little Olive nymphs are thick;

Swimmer mayfly nymphs typical of weed beds on a flat.

hatches of these size sixteen, eighteen, and twenty *Baetis* are often bewildering. Tricos, tiny number twenty-twos and twenty-fours, come off in heavy hatches, stimulating selective feeding on many still summer mornings. The Sulphurs, East and West, populate flats in great numbers; they range from size fourteen to eighteen.

Some large mayflies also inhabit flats. The Western Green Drakes are an example, but their hatches are elusive, subject to whims of wind and weather. It is best to become familiar with the smaller insects that exist in greater numbers, that hatch over longer time periods with daily variations less subject to changes in temperature and rain or sun. If you are prepared to match the smaller but more abundant hatches, when you visit a river to fish its flats you will be prepared for the hatches that are most likely to happen.

Overlapping hatches are common on flats, with two or even three mayfly species coming off at the same time. All of the trout might key on a particular species, ignoring the others. Individual trout might prefer different species, forcing you to pattern a specific fish and determine what species it prefers.

To complicate matters further, there might be two stages of the same species present. While it may appear to the casual observer that a trout takes duns from the surface, it might in reality be feeding on emergers just beneath the surface film.

There are times when terrestrial insects become important on flats. This is especially true on narrow streams with a greater percentage of surface area near the banks that is exposed to chance landings of windblown insects. Ants and beetles are the predominant terrestrial forms along the edges of flats. These are usually tiny, and can be even more frustrating than hatches of small mayflies. But an aquarium net held half in and half out of the surface will strain the current and let you know what fish are taking. Then all you've got to do is calm yourself down and find among your fly boxes the minute pattern that matches the terrestrial and present it correctly to the fussy trout.

Grasshoppers are less frustrating. They often tumble to the surface of a flat. When lots of them suffer the same fate, trout get excited. The resulting dry-fly fishing can be a succession of detonations. It doesn't happen often, but it's fun when it does.

Crustaceans such as scuds and cress bugs are prevalent in waters with a high alkaline content and lots of weed growth. Trout nose into the weeds, startling the crustaceans like quail, gunning them down in the channels between tendrils of weeds. This can create the most difficult fishing of all: the fish work down among the weeds, they take tiny naturals, and they are spooky as hell. I do not often encounter this kind of fishing and I'm glad I don't, since I freely confess that I seldom do well in these situations.

Temperature and Oxygen

In freestone streams, high temperatures and low oxygen levels can be a problem on flats. The shallow water is exposed to the sun, and it is slower, so it is not delivered as quickly to riffles or rapids that might freshen it. Temperatures rise faster on flats than they do on other parts of a stream. Trout are forced into torpor and then into other water types. But this only happens on freestone waters.

A high percentage of fishable flats are found on spring creeks. These arise from the ground at constant temperatures, year round, and carry the coolness of the earth downstream with them for miles. It is rare that temperatures on spring creek flats reach levels that are distressing to trout.

TROUT LIES ON FLATS

Finding likely holding lies on flats is one of the easiest assignments in reading water. Because of their uniform flows, flats carry the same depth right to the edges, and have high banks from which you can scan the water for likely lies, or likely fish.

Weed Beds

The *structure* of a weed bed forms the most obvious lie on a flat. Trout hold wherever weeds are deep enough to give them overhead protection. Beds that are fissured by minor crevices and canyons offer the most potential protection. They are also among the most difficult places to hook trout. You've got to get close in order to find an angle of presentation that keeps your line, leader, and fly clear of the weeds. Yet trout in such water are extremely wary; getting close to them is not nearly as easy as it is in a riffle or run of similar depth.

Fallen jack pines form lots of holding lies on a spring-creek flat.

Obstructions

Any visible shelter or protection is an obvious place to find fish, especially when they are not found feeding elsewhere. Boulders, either protruding or revealed by gentle boils on the surface, are excellent prime lies. It is common to find logs wedged in flats; the current is not always strong enough to dislodge them.

On many narrow western spring creeks, jackstraw tangles of fallen pine trees lie anchored to the banks by their roots, their tops angled downstream by the insistent current. Their limbs form a sanctuary from overhead predation and from carelessly presented flies.

Ledges and Trenches

Ledges and trenches are common features in flats, especially in areas where volcanic activity forms much of the geography of the stream bottom. Trenches form holding lies wherever they are a foot or two deeper than the rest of the flat. At times these lies appear to be crammed with trout, since the entire population that lives across the flat shelters wherever it can when not out feeding. Trenches usually show up on flats as slightly darker areas; sometimes they are revealed by a slick on the surface that is smoother than the rest of the surface of the flat.

Reading water in flats depends to a small extent on your ability to recognize all of the above types of holding lies. But it depends more on your ability to spot rising trout.

Reading water on flats is a matter of locating actively feeding fish, either by their rises or by the almost invisible winks that reveal fish feeding under water. Flats are almost always fished over working trout. They are most challenging then. It is common to see anglers sitting on the banks of such famous rivers as The Henry's Fork or the Firehole, waders on and rods strung, chatting quietly, waiting for the hatch to start before they begin fishing.

Trout activity on flats is almost always tied directly to some form of insect activity. Because water conditions are relatively constant throughout the year, the range of insect species is fairly narrow. But the species best adapted to prevailing conditions will be incredibly abundant. You usually have to match the hatch in order to catch the trout.

STRATEGIES FOR FISHING FLATS

Fishing flats can be just as frustrating as it sounds it could be: trout rise all around you, they give all sorts of clues to what they might be taking, they respond with all sorts of refusals to whatever you are certain will fool them this time. Hope springs eternal. Keep looking, and keep changing flies and tactics.

Observation and change are the elemental secrets to success when fishing flats. Once you learn to observe closely what the fish are taking and change flies and presentations until you match both the insect and its behavior, then you will begin to unravel the mysteries of flats. One of their most charming mysteries is that they do not get unraveled on every occasion. There will always be times when you, or at least when I, cannot solve the prevailing problem, and catch the selective fish.

When trout do not feed actively on flats, you can fish for them in the obvious lies pointed out earlier: around boulders and logs, in trenches or along ledges, and over weed beds. But the most challenging fishing on flats happens when you spot trout working and fish for them with dressings that imitate the naturals they are taking at the time. On those occasions when everything magically weaves together, you will find the most rewarding fishing on flats. As time goes on and you gain experience at this type of fishing, the scarcity of those magic moments diminishes.

Tackle for Fishing Flats

Tackle for flats must be the finest you can acquire; tactics must employ the greatest finesse you can gather. It takes lots of practice to learn to fish flats with more than random success. Even experienced fly fishermen who have achieved their wings on other types of water – riffles, runs, and pools – encounter skunks when first beginning to fish flats.

Your tackle should be fine, with eight-and-a-half to nine-foot rods in the three-, four-, or five-weight class the best. Dry lines suffice for almost all fishing on flats; you will seldom need to get down so deep that you can't do it in the length of a leader. The line can be either a double-taper or a weight-forward, whichever you prefer to use most of the time in other types of fishing. You will need to control your line, but your casts on flats should seldom exceed a length that will allow you to control it comfortably with the forward section of a weight-forward line.

The leader for fishing flats should start at around ten feet long. If you use lead on the leader for nymphing, place it at the end of this, then add a couple of feet of tippet that balances the size fly you have chosen. If you fish emergers or drys, add two more feet of finer tippet, again to balance the fly, and you will have a fourteen-foot leader. That's about the right length to start. You might want it longer. Whatever its length, keep your tippets long, no less than a couple of feet, sometimes three or four feet.

Your tippet will tell on you.

I watched from the top of a high bank recently, waiting with my camera, while Jim Schollmeyer fished over a heavy trout rising steadily on a Bighorn River flat. The insects it took were easy to see; they were a #18 dark caddis, easy to match with a dark Elk Hair Caddis clipped of its bottom hackles.

Jim cast quartering down to the fish, with a slack line. His presentations were perfect. The fly fed out ahead of the line and leader, and should have appeared over the trout with no seeming attachment. But it refused every drift of the fly. Finally Jim stopped casting and started fiddling with his gear.

"Changing flies?" I called down.

"No, changing the tippet from 5X to 6X," he answered.

That's from two-pound to one-pound. I waited to see what would happen. On the first cast the trout rose with great assurance and took the same Elk Hair that had passed over it the same way a dozen times before.

Jim Schollmeyer working for trout on a Bighorn River flat.

The trout instantly ran into the weeds and broke Jim off. It's a common dilemma on flats: sometimes you can't hook trout on a tippet that's stout enough to hold them.

Fishing the Bottom

Fish feeding along the bottom of flats are perhaps the most difficult of all. We do not normally think in terms of selectivity when fish feed deep. In faster water they usually take whatever insect, or reasonable representation of one, tumbles to them on the current.

A couple of conditions make that less likely on flats. First, the narrow range of aquatic insect species, coupled with extreme abundance, makes it common for fish to see nothing but a lot of exactly the same thing. They key in on the insect's shape, size, and color; they won't take anything that doesn't look a lot like it. Second, the slow and clear water on a flat gives trout a good look at whatever they are about to eat. If the imitation is not fairly close and is not presented in the same way the naturals arrive to the trout, they will detect the difference and reject the fly.

Fly selection for fishing the bottom should be based on the most abundant food form available under the water. This is sometimes easy to check out; just reach down and scoop up a handful of weeds. Whatever is most abundant will be crawling around in your hand. But it often happens that what is most abundant is not most available. In such a case it might become necessary to hold a screen net down along the bottom and wait patiently to see what tumbles into it, which will also be what tumbles most often into the view of feeding trout.

You can also accomplish the capture of a sample by fooling a mythical first fish and killing it to examine its stomach contents. Do this only if you have a hankering for a trout dinner and are not in an area where it would be damaging to the trout population to take a fish. Some people feel that it is always damaging to the trout population to kill a trout. It's hard to argue against their logic; certainly it is impossible to argue against the idea that it damages that particular trout.

You might prefer to use a stomach pump to exhume whatever the trout has eaten lately, thereby springing the insects but sparing the fish. I don't. I have never been able to get over the vision of somebody using a similar, but proportionately larger, device on me. Just thinking about it makes me have to pat my tummy to reassure it. If I don't want to kill a trout, I release it with all of its secrets concealed within it. But I can understand why others would do otherwise.

What you are most likely to see, if you use a screen net or can fool a first fish, is something small: a mayfly nymph, a caddis larva, or a crustacean. You should match it as closely as you can, first in size, then in form, finally in color.

Your nymph should be at least slightly weighted to get it down. If the water is deep and has much current, a split shot or some twist-on lead might be needed a foot or two above it to keep it from wafting along a foot or two above the bottom. A strike indicator placed on the leader will help you detect takes, although at times it is possible to observe the flash of white as a trout opens its mouth to take your fly.

It would be easiest to fish flats if you could wade into position straight downstream from feeding fish. This would prevent any chance they might see you. But you cannot cast from there; the sight of line and leader flying overhead would put the fish to fright. You have to stalk carefully into a position off to the side, at an angle from forty-five degrees downstream to a position straight across from the fish.

Cast above the fish far enough to give your nymph a chance to sink down to it. Let the fly dead-drift along the bottom or just above it. Watch your indicator for any hesitation. Be persistent; it is rare to get a perfect presentation on one cast out of five. Even then the fish might have just done in a natural, and will not quite be ready to take again at the instant your fly is ready to be taken.

It requires a lot of observation, and a lot of casts, before you begin to take bottom-feeding fish from flats with anything approaching happy regularity.

Fishing Mid-depths

Because of all the weeds in a flat, its mid-depths are an extension of its bottom. Insects or crustaceans get loose in the drift, in the central layers of the current, when they redistribute their dense populations. They also get taken at mid-depths on their way to the surface for emergence. In either case, it is important to determine just what stage of what creature is attracting the attention of the trout. Once that is determined you should imitate it with a traditional wet fly, a soft-hackled wet fly, or a small nymph.

You will almost always fish mid-depths at the prompting of trout visibly feeding. You can fish upstream, the same way you would fish the bottom. But leave off the lead and shorten the distance between indicator and fly so the imitation passes through the water at the depth of the feeding trout. Take up a position at an angle downstream from the fish, or straight across from them, so your fly is presented to them at the end of the cast, on a straight leader, without anything alarming passing over their heads.

You can also present your flies at mid-depths from upstream. You will have to wade into position more carefully. Work to where your cast is angled forty-five to sixty degrees downstream to the fish. Mark a single rising fish. Cast above and beyond its position, let the fly sink, then coax it into swimming slowly right in front of the nose of the fish. With any luck you will feel a slight tightening as the line bellies down in the current. Set the hook by raising the rod gently or you will jerk the fly away from the fish.

Fishing the Surface

There are two slightly separate levels to consider when fishing the surface of a flat. First, there is the moment during emergence when the natural insect reaches the surface film. It will suspend for a few seconds and trout sometimes feed selectively on this stage of the natural during a hatch. You see the adults on the surface, but you do not see the emergers just beneath it. Second, there is the adult stage itself, after the emerger has penetrated the film and cast its cuticle. When trout concentrate on this stage, true dry-fly fishing is at its most challenging.

If you fail to separate the two stages and fish the wrong one, you are in for fishing that is not challenging but frustrating. Fishing flats requires more observation than any other trout-fishing situation.

The tackle and tactics for the two kinds of fishing are exactly the same. The only difference is in the flies you use. Emerger dressings should be extensions of nymphs, with small wing clumps of fur or polypropylene yarn added to represent the half-extruded wings of the natural. These flies were covered in *Handbook of Hatches,* and you should see that book for more detailed notes on them.

When fishing dry flies on flats your imitations should be the most exact you can either tie or buy. Trout are not likely to accept dressings that are two color shades off, or two hook sizes large. Nor are they going to be delighted by presentations that are made with gear that is too coarse to fish on flats.

An upstream presentation of a dry fly or an emerger on a glassy flat will accomplish one major event: it will deliver the fly to the fish after the line and leader have already passed over its head twice and astonished it once. The best presentation on smooth water requires wading into position *upstream* from the fish, remembering to keep a profile low enough that they cannot see you. The fly should be delivered downstream, with slack tossed into the cast so the line lands on the water with the "S" shape of a swimming snake. The S's swim out as the current draws the fly down toward the fish, and the fly passes over the fish first, with no drag.

Because this kind of fishing is not of much use when merely covering the water, hoping to raise fish, it is best to cast to an individual rising trout. Pattern its rises and present your fly so that it lands a foot or two above the trout just at the time it is ready to rise again. The fly drifts over the fish ahead of line and leader. If the fish refuses, tilt the rod over to the side, let the current draw the line away from the trout's feeding lane, then lift the fly and cast again. And again and again and again.

It takes a lot of casts before everything becomes perfect and the trout rises gullibly to the fly.

9

Probing Pocket Water

Any object that interrupts the current forms a quiet bit of water where a trout can hold a station with a window on a territory that feeds it well. Most prime lies in riffles and runs are pieces of pocket water, in a way. But in this chapter I want to treat the kinds of prime lies that are more commonly considered when we use the term *pocket water.*

Pocket water is any quiet hesitation that holds trout in the midst of water that is too fast and too turbulent for them to remain anywhere else for more than a brief time. Riffles and runs have pockets of quiet water, but the water around them is usually not quite so brutal that trout can't hold in it when given a good motive, such as a lucrative hatch of insects.

Pocket water, as it is defined here, is found in rapids and cascades. The current in these water types is so swift that trout cannot survive long without something to hide behind. Remember that a trout tires of constant fast swimming in less than five minutes. A trout fighting frantic water would have to swim urgently upstream to keep from being delivered downstream like an aquatic insect on the drift.

Structure of Pocket Water

Pocket water is found only where the flow has a steep gradient. But steep water is not restricted to mountainsides. Almost all streams have stretches that bolt through gorges or rush down through tumbles of rock with lots of rapids and cascades. Most trout streams offer pocket fishing, and it will usually be good fishing because pocket water is so difficult to fish that most fishermen avoid it.

We tend to think of boulders when we think of quiet spots in water like this. Boulders are the most common cause of pockets that hold trout, simply because something like a log or limb rarely gets a chance to set down its roots in such fast water.

Boulders of sufficient size to form holding lies usually protrude from the water. They sit out there calmly with water rushing all around them, stained white by bird poop on their tops. The water piles against their upstream sides, gives up and swings around them and leaves an eddy in its wake. The eddy is a swirl on the surface, but there is at least one quiet spot down beneath it, usually right on the bottom, where a trout can rest and wait for insects and other forms of food to tumble by.

There are also ledges and trenches in fast water. Some slice across the current, marked by a line of white water followed by a patch of quiet water. Some run parallel to the current; these are marked by brief slicks in the fast water.

An occasional abrupt leveling in the steep gradient of a rapid will also slow the water, creating a very brief pocket-run in the

Pocket-water lies in a mountain stream.

midst of water that tumbles brutally above, below, and off to both sides of it. These look remarkably like miniature runs, with level tops and unbroken flows for ten to perhaps thirty feet. Because the water around them is rough, they are normally quiet spots in the storm, but not as smooth on top as they would be if they were surrounded by quiet water. You've got to look carefully to separate them from what's around them.

The size of a piece of pocket water depends first on the size of the stream, second on the size of the structure that forms the pocket in the stream. A giant boulder in a large river might make a pocket twice the size of the largest plunge pool in a mountain creek. A piece of pocket water in a mountain creek, in contrast, might hide behind a boulder the size of a basketball and give you a casting target no bigger than a basketball hoop.

THE NEEDS OF TROUT

The needs of trout are met in pockets in largely the same ways they are met in the prime lies of riffles and runs. Shelter is usually the limiting factor to the value of a holding lie. That is especially true in pocket water. Trout hold only where they find water still enough to give them comfort.

The obstruction that causes a pocket gives trout shelter from the swift current. The upwelling of water above the obstruction is not often slow enough to form a pillow of slow water; the best holding water is almost always found immediately downstream, deep along the bottom.

A ledge or shelf large enough to be reflected to the surface as a bit of calm water will also have enough quiet water down below to shelter a trout or two. Sometimes a pod of trout will hold in a fairly large trench, one that is ten to twenty feet long and two to three feet deeper than the water around it. When you get into a patch of this kind of water, you can catch half a dozen trout in the same number of casts, all the time wondering why you are suddenly such a superb fisherman. It's because you read the water right.

Protection from predators is excellent in pocket water. The surface is too broken for vision from above; the water is too broken for predation from below. Even angling predation is discouraged by the kind of wading needed to fish pocket water right.

If a pocket is large enough to provide shelter for a trout, it is almost sure to be large enough to provide food for it, too. The fast and oxygen-rich water of a rapid or cascade can be kind to insects. The bottom has lots of crevices and spaces where nymphs and larvae find protection from the current. Because the water is swift, lots of these get knocked loose and delivered in the drift.

During the warmer months, when fish and fishermen are both most active, insects that have reached maturity constantly migrate out of fast water in preparation for emergence where the water is more congenial. They arrive in pockets for the same reason the trout hold there: for shelter from the white water around the pocket. They need a safe place to perform their emergence.

They are safe from the current when emerging in pocket water, but they are not safe from the trout.

Trout foods in pocket water are primarily aquatic insects. Mayfly nymphs in rapids and cascades belong to the clinging variety, with some crawlers holding on as best they can. The predominant species fall in the medium range of sizes, twelve to fourteen.

Most caddisfly larvae that live in fast water construct their cases of sand and pebbles. The ballast of the heavy material holds them down on the bottom, which is where they want to be. They are generally medium-to-large insects, sizes eight to twelve.

Stonefly nymphs adapted to fast water are generally the large salmon fly and golden stone varieties, adapted well to crawling about among the stones, but poor swimmers when they are dislodged by brisk currents. They are the primary reason that #6 and #8 nymphs work well when pitched right to the bottom of pocket water.

All of these types of insects move into the relatively calm water of pockets when it is their time to emerge. Trout see fairly heavy numbers of a single species at times, but it is rare that they become selective. Fast water, and the fractious way it delivers drift, gives a trout little time to light up its pipe and think things over when a promising bit of flotsam passes its way. The trout must dash for it, grab it, and make a decision about its edibility

Stonefly nymphs are typical inhabitants of pocket water.

after its flight has been contained. You have to be alert, and set the hook quickly, when fishing pocket water. Trout are used to spitting things out.

If the stream is narrow, quite a few terrestrial insects find their unhappy way into the drift. Many are taken under the water after they've drowned. When terrestrials are most abundant, though, trout focus on the surface and cock their fins, ready to race up and spear a beetle, termite, or inchworm before it gets swept away.

Oxygen and temperature regimes are obviously excellent in pocket water. If trout are forced by a summer heat wave to pack their bags and move out of one water type to find comfort in another, pocket water is where they will go. Under these conditions, especially if there are poorly oxygenated pools nearby, you sometimes find pocket water holding a richness of trout that will astonish you.

HOLDING LIES IN POCKET WATER

Any pocket that holds trout in fast water forms a prime lie, meeting all of the needs of the trout in that one place. The size of the trout will be directly related to the size of the pocket and to the amount of food that it gathers. The bigger the pocket, the bigger the fish.

Reading pocket water is a two-pronged affair of looking for obstructions in the current and learning to spot slight slicks and eddies that indicate still pockets beneath the current. One easy way to think about the fishability of a pocket you are scoping is to envision a bushy dry-fly cast to its surface: if the water is gentle enough that the fly would get a good float, even if only for a foot or two, the pocket is large enough that it might hold a trout. If the water descends so harshly onto an obstruction that it tears whitely around it and no fly would float behind it, then it is unlikely that a trout could hold there, either.

STRATEGIES FOR FISHING POCKET WATER

Trout are always on their stations in pocket water, hanging tight along the bottom, in the water just downstream from whatever obstructs the current. They are nearly always prepared to feed. The distance they will move to take a fly depends on the depth of the water, its vigor, and any insect activity that has rewarded them recently so that they are inclined to move and feed.

Tackle for Pocket Water

Tackle chosen to fish pocket water should be what you would choose to fish the rest of the same stream. Pockets are opportunity water; few streams have pocket water as the dominant form of holding lies. You want to be prepared to fish them when you come to them. But you don't necessarily want to go to a stream just to pick its pockets unless it has lots of neglected pocket water, which holds lots of neglected trout. Then it's worth it.

If you are prepared to fish the riffles and runs of the creek, stream, or river you are on, you will also be prepared to fish its pockets. Everything tends to be relative. But pockets and pools have one thing in common: if you are lightly armed for the rest of the water, it will show up as a handicap when you approach a pool or a piece of pocket water.

If a rod were chosen just to probe pockets, it should be long, and stout enough to be bossy. The line should be a six-weight for small streams, a seven or eight for larger water. You will want to command heavy flies with it. There is no difference between double-taper and weight-forward lines, because all of your casts will be short. The line should be a floater for all but the deepest pocket water. If a pocket is too deep to probe with a floating line and an eight- to ten-foot leader, then switch to a super-fast-sinking wet-tip line, and shorten the leader to three or four feet.

Tippets should always be heavy enough to turn over fairly large flies, and strong enough to hold trout against strong currents. Four- to six-pound-test is about right on small to medium water. Use six- to eight-pound points on larger rivers, where you expect larger fish.

Fishing the Bottom

The bottom is the most likely level to probe first in pocket water, unless the water is shallow and lots of insects are active. In that case a dry fly might be most effective. Dry-fly fishing might be most fun at all times, and there is nothing wrong with pecking away at pocket water with a dry even when it is not the most effective method. I do it all the time.

When fishing the bottom, use weighted nymphs. Select the size based on your estimation of the typical trout foods you think might drift into the pockets. On small streams, use flies in the #10 to #12 size range. On medium and large streams, where you would expect the trout to go for larger bites, use nymphs tied on #6 and #8 hooks. The dressings should be standard searching patterns: Zug Bugs, Gold-Ribbed Hare's Ears, Gray Nymphs, and an occasional giant salmon fly nymph imitation.

Present the fly near the bottom and as close behind the obstruction that forms the pocket as you can possibly get it. Getting it to plunge swiftly might require some extra lead wrapped on the leader, above the fly. A strike indicator is a help in this type of

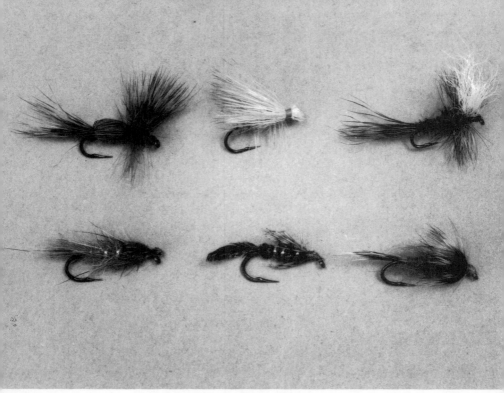

Flies for fishing the top and bottom of pocket water.

fishing. But conflicting currents in pocket water often draw an indicator under water. There is no substitute for fishing as close as you can to the pocket, which allows you to keep in close touch with your fly.

Wading is difficult in and around pocket water. But if you reach a point from which you can loft your rod almost over the pocket, you will be able to keep your line off the water. The fly will sink faster if it is impeded only by the leader, not by the line. And you will be able to direct the drift of the fly by steering it with the rod. This increases the chance of getting a strike and enhances the chance you will learn about it when it happens. If you keep direct contact between the rod top and the fly, a hit to a pocket nymph will be telegraphed to your hand by a sharp rap.

This kind of fishing is almost like dapping, but it's done with a heavy nymph instead of a dry fly. Because the water is turbulent all around a pocket, you can wade into a close position without scaring the fish. But do not wade into the pocket itself. It is better to approach from downstream, or off to the side, than it is to wade in from above. Dirt and debris kicked up by your feet put fish off their feed.

Cast to all of the water that looks like it is peaceful enough to hold a trout. In small pockets this might require only half a dozen casts. In large pockets you should fish the water with a pattern that covers all of the likely places a trout might hold. Fish patiently enough to show the fly to any fish that might be down there. You had to wade hard to get into position to fish the pocket; don't take a couple of casts and then burn up energy forging on to the next pocket. Fish this one out first, then move on to the next promising water.

Fishing Mid-depths

Fish the mid-depths of pocket water only if some sort of insect activity indicates that it would be effective to do so. A hatch of mayflies or a dance of caddis over the pockets might indicate that trout are visited by lots of drift down below. In this case use a wet fly or a small nymph fished on a dry line. Lengthen your casts a little; it helps to be upstream a bit so you can fish downstream at a slight angle to the pocket.

Cast just above and beyond the obstruction that forms the pocket. Let the fly drift down to it. If it is a boulder sticking up above the surface, mend your line over it, then coax the fly around as close as you can behind it. Let the fly swirl in the eddy. Hold your rod high to keep the line off the water, so it won't pull the fly out of holding water. Watch the water closely; takes in this kind of fishing are often visible, with a flash of light as the fish turns, or a splash if it takes near the surface.

You can fish wet flies effectively upstream, working your way from pocket to pocket, casting short and watching your line tip for any hesitation as the fly drifts back down toward you. It is a little like dry-fly fishing, but it is a lot more demanding. It works well where the pockets are no more than two to three feet deep, at times when the fish are unwilling to come all the way to the surface for dry flies. I have found upstream wet-fly fishing most effective when the sun is out and bright on the water.

Fishing the Surface

I've always written that we fish for surprise. Drys bobbing on pocket water provide many of angling's ultimate moments. Drys are also the most effective way to take trout from lots of pockets. They always work best where the water is shallow, two to three feet deep, and when insects are active.

Dry flies for pocket water should be chosen for a high ride and bright visibility. Royal Wulffs and Humpies in sizes eight to twelve are traditional favorites. Elk Hair Caddis work well in sizes ten and twelve. Stimulators, which imitate stoneflies, draw up lots of trout when used in sizes six through ten. All of these float well and show up well to both the angler above and the trout below.

Finesse is not the first requirement in this kind of fishing. Getting the fish to see your fly is more important. Smacking the fly to the water will sometimes announce its arrival to the trout. It helps if you can hold as much line off the water as possible. Wade close, cast short, and keep your fly tap-dancing on the eddied water behind a rock as long as you can get it to stay there.

Safety is always a concern when fishing pocket water. Carry a wading staff. I like a folding staff that fits in a belt holster. It is out of the way until I'm teetering and need it. Then I draw it like a sword and stab the bottom at the last instant to save myself from tipping over. I haven't been nominated for knighthood yet, but neither have I gone swimming in a rapid or a cascade. I don't like rigid staffs because they are always tangled between my legs. When they are not on duty saving me, they are busy trying to trip me.

It's best to avoid getting tripped in white water. It's never fun, and it can be fatal. Wear chest waders with a wading belt, and felt-soled wading boots that are solid enough to protect your feet from constant pounding. If the boulders are slick, a sign that they are rich in feed for insects, wear some sort of cleats that cut through the algae. Wade slowly, planting each foot before moving the other.

You take a chance every time you fish this kind of water. Never increase the risk by wading where you shouldn't. Lots of pocket water is so formidable that it is simply sanctuary water for trout. Leave it at that. You can always catch the trout later, when they've grown so large pocket-water territories no longer sustain them and they have to migrate to the pools down below, where you can get at them.

10

Trout Lies Along
the Banks

Banks are the transition zone between the aquatic and terrestrial environments. The narrow bit of water that abuts against a bank gets enriched from both directions. Aquatic insects migrate in from the stream to emerge next to shore. Terrestrial insects nose out from streamside shrubs and grasses, pitching to the water more often than they prefer. Trout hold along the edges, feeding on all the local abundance of both kinds of insects.

Good bank water is revealed by a combination of three factors that meet the three basic needs of trout: it has indentations or obstructions to shelter trout from the current; it has enough depth to give trout some protection from predators; it has a fair current to deliver food to the trout. Once you learn to recognize banks where these three factors come together, it does not take long to learn to read productive water and to eliminate water that will not hold fish.

THE NEEDS OF TROUT

The needs of trout are met generously along many types of stream banks. They are not met at all along a lot of others. An

angler who does not know the needs of trout and cannot recognize how the water might fulfill those needs can waste a lot of time fishing water that is empty of trout. An angler who can read bank water can make a lot of casts in a day, over very productive water, without ever getting his feet wet.

The need for shelter from currents is well met by indentations in the bank that let trout get out of the flow of the current. Banks that provide this sort of cover usually have a good bit of vegetation. Grassy banks have undercuts beneath them and bites taken out of them. Both kinds of cover shelter trout. Bunchgrass clumps often sweep out over the water, forming good lies downstream. Willow patches sometimes spring from a single ball of roots. The root ball breaks the current; the overhanging limbs drop a constant supply of awkward insects, making trout even happier to be there.

Rocks and boulders under the water also break the current and provide holding lies. Banks with this kind of shelter are usually steep, and the depth of the water falls away quickly to between three and six feet or more into a fast current. Boulders that break the current immediately adjacent to the edge hold trout on both the upstream and downstream sides.

The need for protection from predators is met by depth, at least a foot and a half of it, preferably from two to four feet. The same need can occasionally be met in shallower water by over-hanging vegetation or by shade that falls directly on the water, but depth is the primary factor in protecting trout from overhead predation. Lack of depth is one of the primary signs of empty water: where the bank slopes away gradually, only inches deep, it seldom holds trout.

The need for food is met along banks from both directions. Terrestrials are not the only form of food that arrives from land-ward. Most adult aquatic insects spend their few restful days right along the banks, often falling to the water. All of the fe-males must return to the water to lay their eggs.

Trout foods along banks tend to be caddisflies and stoneflies in spring, caddisflies and mixed terrestrials in early summer, cad-disflies and grasshoppers in late summer, and mostly caddisflies in fall. When some other insect is dominant, it is best to go with an imitation of it. When no other insect is dominant, it is best to go with something that trout can mistake for a caddis.

The need for food is not satisfied unless there is a moderate-to-brisk current to deliver whatever falls to the water to trout wait-ing downstream. You rarely find trout holding along banks that have no current at all.

STRUCTURE OF BANKS

Not all streams have a lot of good bank water. The more stable the flow of a river, the more bank water it will offer. A river subject to high run-off and low summer flows will have wider gravel bars and less fishable bank water.

Meadow streams tend to work their deepest water up against the banks, and it takes water with depth to make good bank fishing. Tailwater fisheries below dams, where the flow is rela-tively stable, have many reaches with good banks. But even free-stone streams, subject to spring spates and summer droughts, offer fine banks on the outsides of bends. Sometimes this coincides with a bend pool, and the deep water along the bank holds some of the largest trout in the stream.

Good banks on meadow streams tend to be recognized as excellent water; they are often fished hard. But banks on freestone rivers are seldom fished. Sometimes there are good reasons for this: it is often murderous to make your way in to the best bank water on a typical gravel-bar stream.

TROUT LIES ALONG BANKS

There are several tip-offs to the kind of bank water that is worth struggling to get to. An undercut bank is an obvious one, especially on an outside bend that has sides falling steeply to the water. Hummocks of bunchgrass or clumps of willows increase the chances that this will be productive water, since their root systems grip the soil and form overhangs and indentations. Gentle boils working along the bank indicate rocks just under the water and increase the number of lies for trout.

Manmade riprap banks are almost always productive. They are in place to stabilize the stream banks and are seldom wasted where the currents are not brisk. They are improved wherever the rock was dumped casually, allowed to roll down the bank and settle as it might. The resulting underwater jumble has lots of prime lies. Riprap is not so fine where it is prettily laid like a paving-stone roadway tipped on its side, half in and half out of the water. These banks have few holding lies.

Natural rock banks, caused by tumbles of boulders off the hills above the water, are prime banks wherever they have a fair current sweeping along them. But natural rockfalls are wasted if they step off into still water. Of course, if the water in such a case is more than five or six feet deep, it might be good as a pool, and the tumbled boulders will increase that chance. But it should be fished with tactics described for pools, not for banks.

Riffles rarely have productive banks unless they flow through narrow slots and hold their depth right against the shore. Most riffles have shallow, sloped banks, and trout hold farther out. Runs often have productive banks, with the water a couple of feet deep and flowing well right against the shore. Wherever

The author's father lands a trout while fishing dry-shod along a riprap bank on the Deschutes River.

such water has sufficient indentations or breaks to the current under the surface, you will find trout.

Pools, as mentioned above, can be good bank water if they are deep right to the edges. But it is usually most productive to fish them from the inside of the curve, wading in shallow water and casting long toward the outside bank. Normal pool tactics work well in these situations, and bank tactics are rarely the best bet. They should be employed only where the pool is so wide that you can't wade the shallow side and cast far enough to reach the deep side.

Flats usually have excellent bank water, though it is also usually overlooked. Where a flat keeps its even depth to the very edge, the banks will often be the most productive water because of all the food that gathers there. But anglers tend to concentrate on the hatches that happen in the open water of a flat, fussing over the mayflies and midges that emerge there. That is the way it should be; flats are supposed to be frustrating. But turn your back on those rising fish long enough to examine the transition line and you are likely to find fish rising there, too. Sometimes they are larger; sometimes they are feeding on a potpourri of aquatic and terrestrial insects and are less selective. But sometimes they are feeding on terrestrial minutiae, and then they will drive you back out into open water, where things are simpler.

Pocket water might not be considered a feature of banks. But often there are pockets in swift water that you dare not wade but can reach with a cast from the banks. There are places on many tumbling reaches of river where the biggest trout are picked out from behind boulders near shore, while the water out away from shore, out of casting range, is so brutal its fish are absolutely safe.

Unproductive banks are usually defined by the absence of one of the three prime factors: current, shelter, and depth. It takes all three to make good bank water.

Where water sweeps around an outside bend against a steep dirt bank, it commonly looks productive but fails to give up a fish. The reason is the lack of indentations and boulders to provide shelter from the current. The inside of a bend is usually a gravel bar that slopes too gently, not attaining enough depth to protect trout from predators until it is too far out to be considered a bank. And there are miles of bank on any stream where the water simply lacks sufficient current to make it attractive to trout.

STRATEGIES FOR FISHING BANKS

Trout, when they are found along the banks, are like Napoléon: they have not come to make a speech, Josephine. They are there to feed. They are accustomed to making quick decisions. Because most of the feed along the transition line arrives from above, they are eager to ambush dry flies. Because their supply lines seldom consistently provide an identical grocery from one moment to the next, they are not usually selective.

Successful tactics for fishing banks call first for working your way into a good position to present your flies. This sometimes means you will have to fight brush and briers and even worse.

Rick Hafele, author of *Aquatic Insects and Their Imitations,* fished the Deschutes with me last May. He came back to camp for lunch one day with eyes that were rather round. I asked him what had happened.

"I got to going down a gravel bank to the river too fast," he told me, waving his arms. "I started skidding. I heard something buzzing and looked down. A rattlesnake and I were on a collision course. I managed to backpedal and tread gravel. It must have been hurrying for its hole; it dove underground and disappeared." If that snake was as excited as Rick, it's probably still down its hole, waving its own arms, telling its friends about its narrow escape.

Tackle for Fishing Banks

Most bank fishing is dry-fly fishing, and your tackle should be chosen with that in mind. Gear for fishing drys along the banks should be fairly standard for fishing dry flies anywhere. I use an eight-foot rod with a quick action, balanced to a five-weight double-taper line, for most of my bank fishing. It is the same rod I use for most of my other fishing, and I am naturally armed with it when I approach a bank. Most people prefer rods a foot longer. They are an advantage for lifting a backcast over high bankside grass, a disadvantage for wriggling through bankside brush. I do a lot of wriggling, so I like the shorter rod. You suit yourself.

The leader should be about the length of the rod, tapered to a tippet that turns the fly over briskly. I seldom go below four-pound-test, simply because I fish where the currents are strong, the fish sometimes large, and the banks so brushy I can seldom follow a fish when it runs. I want to be able to hold it, and later to bring it upstream to land it. I can't do that when the trout weighs a couple of pounds and my tippet is in the same class.

Fishing the Bottom

Fishing the bottom along the banks can be effective at the edges of runs or where you want to probe a few pockets near

The author's dad probing indentations and boulders along a grassy bank with a dry fly.

shore without wading out to them. This kind of fishing should be done with large weighted nymphs, lobbed with the kind of gear appropriate for them. You should move slowly, either working your way along the shoreline or wading so near to the bank that you can reach out and grab it if you start to tip over into deeper water.

It is best to fish upstream, but there will be places where you can only enter through the brush to an access above a likely holding lie. In this case make a short cast downstream, then feed line into the drift of the fly so that it drifts as naturally as possible. You will rarely get a perfect drift, but you will often get a good whack anyway.

Fishing Mid-depths

Fishing mid-depths is not particularly productive along banks. It is usually better to fish either on the bottom or on the top.

Fishing the Surface

The food along banks is largely surface fare, and fish normally hold there with the attitude that they would be happy to jump upward for a dry fly. It is by far the most pleasant way to fish along banks. It is also usually the most productive.

The Elk Hair Caddis in sizes ten to fourteen is my favorite dressing for poking along the banks. I find that it works very well when caddis are out, which is intermittently all season long. I also find that it works well when stoneflies are out, when hoppers are hopping, and when a variety of minor terrestrials go plopping to the water. Other good dressings are the Royal Wulff and Stimulator, but if you have a pattern in which you have more faith than mine, stick with it. The trout will probably like it unless they are onto something particular, in which case you might want to match it.

Presentation of dry flies should be tight against the banks. Given a good boulder or an eddy, bank water might be five feet out. But most of the time the best bank water is within a foot of shore. Casts more than three feet from shore should be to specific lies that you have spotted and suspect might hold a wicked trout. In most situations, cast with a pattern that covers the water at the bank, then a foot out, then two feet out, and finally three feet out. Fish any lies beyond that as lies, with targeted casts.

Within the bankside zone, there will be many features that you want to give special attention. Place your fly close into the opening of any indentation. Cast below, to the outside, and above any clump of bunchgrass that hangs over the water. Do the same with any boulder. In all but the fastest water, I take more fish above boulders than I do below. Cast as far as you can up under any willow or alder limbs that sweep to the water.

After you have fished out a few feet of bank, move forward and fish the next few feet. Fish upstream, with casts as short as you can.

Eddies are special bankside water. Some are tiny, and you

should fish these in the course of your upstream ambulations. But some are ten to twenty feet across, especially where a strong current swings out away from shore. In these kinds of eddies, the water along the bank flows upstream instead of down, and trout holding along the bank face into the current, which means they face downstream. You should back away from the bank, approach the lower end of the upstream-flowing eddy, and then fish the bank against the current, with the fish facing away from you.

Large eddies are traps for all sorts of aquatic debris, including insects. Trout sometimes feed selectively on the surface, hanging in pods because territoriality gets suspended in the slow water of eddies. They are dark ghosts just under the water about a foot and a half long, or big noses a couple of inches across, poking out of the water to take something so small you can't even see it.

Eddies are maddening situations. But if you are patient enough, you can work into position and wait for the fish to settle down and get used to your presence. Then use an aquarium net, or scan the water with binoculars, to see what they are picking from the current. Match it if you can. Extend your tippet four feet or so. Present the fly with no more than a flick of your rod tip; anything more will put the trout down again.

When trout feed selectively in eddies along the banks, you have to apply the tactics of flats. You must contrive to place the fly *upstream* from a rising fish with lots of slack in the leader. As the slack feeds out, the fly will be delivered to the trout; the two-inch nose will reappear to inspect your fly. It might take it under with it. It can happen, but it won't happen often. Most of the time the fly will be rejected. Success in eddies takes a lot of practice, and a lot of patience.

It also takes a lot of luck. There are a thousand conflicting and invisible currents on the surface of every eddy. You can put everything together just right and the whim of the water can tear it all apart in a second and put the trout down and make you wait until they come up once more and get used to things and start feeding all over again. Trout in eddies can be alarmingly difficult. They make you want to stomp off and fish a riffle.

Fishing the banks from boats is another special situation. I'll lay down a few rules here, and let you learn the rest from your guide, who will want to yell at you but won't, if you screw up, because his reputation and therefore his livelihood depends on your catching fish. The first rule is this: Don't ever look at the scenery. Don't look up, you're bound to miss a strike.

Fishing water like Montana's beautiful Bitterroot can be a confusing situation. You want to watch all the mountains and cottonwoods and tall clouds float by, but you want to catch a three-pound brown, too. Sometimes you wish you were rowing the boat so the guide could stare at his fly while you enjoyed the scenery. But try to work out a balance. Flick your eyes to the water ahead. This is one of the rewards for learning to recognize empty water: when you see some coming, steal a glance at Montana and hope you've learned it right. If a fish comes up out of that empty water and takes your fly while your gaze is uplifted, your guide is going to shout, and you can't blame me.

Reading water becomes doubly important when fishing from a

Doc Hughes sizing up the cast to a boulder-lie while boat fishing along the banks of the Madison.

boat: you don't have a lot of time to analyze the best lies, and you have to hit the best lies or you'll capture the worst trout.

Recall the three factors of good bank water, *current speed, depth,* and *shelter.* Wherever you see these things converging, plunk your fly down quickly. If nothing comes to it in a hurry, get it out of there and plunk it down in the next place where all three things come together. A boat moves so fast that you will probably only be able to hit every third piece of bank that you recognize as a prime lie. But that's all right; if you can read the water you can hit your share of them. If you can't read the water, you won't fish nearly as much good water as bad. Always remember that there is a lot more bad water than there is good water.

When fishing with streamers or nymphs, cast at an angle behind the boat. As soon as the fly lands, start to strip it out. The boat, farther out in the stream, is in faster water, moving away from the fly. This helps you keep a tight line so you can feel a strike and get the hook into the fish. The worst sin when boat fishing with sunk flies is letting a lot of slack get into your line so you can't tell when you have a take. If you cast ahead of the boat, you'll have to retrieve at a sprint to keep slack out of the line.

If you fish dry, cast at an angle ahead of the boat. Again, the boat is out in faster water than the fly, and as it slowly catches up it will increase the slack in the line and give your fly a longer effective float. Gradually gather the line that goes slack; when a fish hits, you want to have close enough contact with your fly to set the hook. If you cast behind the boat with a dry fly, you will have drag almost instantly.

Whether you fish from a boat or from the bank, remember that bank water is *tight against the bank,* not five feet away from it. Keep your flies in the prime lies and you will take your share of fish from banks.

11

Special Techniques for Mountain Creeks

Mountain creeks are special places for me. I grew up fishing the forested hills along the coast of Oregon. The tiny streams bound whitely down to the Pacific Ocean. Wherever waterfalls block upstream migrations of salmon and steelhead, the pools in the secret headwaters above the falls hide bands of bold and hungry cutthroat trout.

Creeks offer isolation. But more important to the angler seeking lessons in reading water, they offer an intimacy that you don't get on larger streams. Small creeks have an abundance of fish and though they are small like their streams, they are always willing to tell you if you have taken your lessons well.

The type of terrain dictates the nature of a stream. Most mountain creeks have steep gradients, tumbling down swiftly until they gather others of their kind, slow a bit, and become the larger trout streams down below that we fish most of the time. But most also have gentler stretches, mellowing a bit for a half mile or more. A few even have meadow-stream reaches.

The structure of the streambed is dictated by the nature of

the stream. The higher into the headwaters you go, the less the effects of erosion, and the more likely the rocks will be large. On my favorite coastal mountain creek I am constantly forced to climb boulders bigger than the pickup that delivered me over the old logging roads and to the lip of the canyon far above the creek bottom.

The important holding lies in creeks are almost always plunge pools, short runs, brief tailouts of runs and pools, or pocket-water lies amid cascades. Water types that are relatively rare include riffles, flats, and bank water, though on the narrowest creeks, using the widest definitions, it's almost all bank water.

Few of the needs of trout are met generously on mountain creeks. The need for shelter is met in the plunge pools and the short runs. But there are long stretches of cascading water where only an occasional boulder or log breaks the flow enough for a trout to hold behind it. The winter and spring brutality of a

Typical plunge pool on a small mountain creek.

mountain creek, when the water is high, reduces the number of sheltering places to a very few, and might be the limiting factor to the number of trout that survive until summer.

The need for protection from predators is satisfied to a certain extent by the many large boulders and ledges beneath which the trout can hide. But when they come out to feed they are exposed, usually in shallow water. The nearness of overhanging branches on a narrow waterway increases the danger from patient kingfishers. I never fish my favorite streams without startling, and being startled by, one or two of these raucous hunters.

The need for food is met rather sparsely on most mountain creeks. That is one of the reasons their trout are so eager for your flies: they are always hungry.

The types of food are extremely varied. Most aquatic insects have adapted to niches within creeks. There are mayflies, stoneflies, caddisflies, midges, alderflies, and other flies. Variety is a sign of the health of a stream: diversity of insect species reports a healthy environment; a narrow list of species tells you something is wrong, and likely tells you that we did it. But all this variety makes it rare that any one insect is dominant. That is why you seldom match a hatch on a small mountain creek. An attractor dressing will almost always incite the fish to strike.

Terrestrial insects are important in relation to the width of a stream. The narrower it is, the higher the proportion of them that make their way into the stream's drift. Creeks, with their overshadowing conifers and alders, are rich in landborne insects: beetles, carpenter ants, termites, leafhoppers, and inchworms. Trout see such a wide variety of them that they do not become selective to any one of them.

Territoriality is an important factor on the smallest streams. Prime holding lies are few, and usually small. The size of the territory dictates the amount of food a fish will see and is one of the major factors limiting the size of the trout caught on small streams. Catch one that stands above the others in size, and the size of the lie from which you caught it will also almost always stand out above the rest of those in the stream. That is one reason reading water is important on small streams. It also provides a way you can learn more about reading water: if you begin to notice what kind of water gives up the largest trout, you will quickly learn to notice where the three needs of trout are met in one spot.

Trout in creeks usually hold on stations, watching territories for drift. If conditions are such that much feed is delivered to them, they rest on cocked fins, ready to race for any promising bite that lands on the water near them. They feed on the drift at all levels, since all the levels are normally so close together.

"Fish those current tongues," I was constantly advised by my mentors, when I first began fishing tiny streams. "That's where the trout hold. Right under the current tongues. Ignore the rest of the water." For years I did as I was told, fishing only the frothed water where cascades plunged into pools. And I caught lots of fish, more and more as I learned how to cast better, and learned to tie dry flies that floated better. But it began to intrigue me that I saw so many dark ghosts of fish fleeing up from the tailouts as soon as I entered pools.

Finally I ignored my advisors. I began taking a few preliminary casts at the tailout of each pool before I poked my head up to where any trout holding there could see me. This was frustrating fishing at first. It's easy to get a good float on a current tongue. All you have to do is pop your fly to it and it will drift naturally back down toward you. But a tailout is another matter entirely. It is slow water, gathering to drop into the rush of water below. Your fly lands where the water creeps, but your line lands on that rush below, and almost immediately you have drag. Even a small-stream trout bolts when a fly speedboats across the top of its shallow tailout.

After some time I learned to cast from an off angle, so that most of my line landed on the bank, with only the leader and fly on the water. Or I learned to hook my casts, so the fly came in where I wanted it, but the line looped off to the side and landed on land. As you can see, I fish truly narrow creeks. Eventually I learned to use protruding rocks, casting so the fly landed on the tailout and the line crossed a dry rock below it. The fly would get a natural float, and I would often get a fish.

I was astonished to learn that the larger fish held in the lower water, and that as the season wore on, and the water dropped lower and lower, more and more good fish held on the tailouts and in the still parts of the pools. The reason is evident in hindsight: in spring, most of the feed is aquatic insects, which arrive from the fast water above, and the prime place for a trout to hold is at the head of a pool. But as the season heats up, most of the feed becomes terrestrial life, dropped from above, and the prime lie becomes the point from which a trout can keep an eye on the largest part of the surface of the pool. That, of course, is from the tailout.

My mentors, who advised me to fish only the current tongues, fished only in May and June. Then they gave the streams up as too low to fish. I crouch lower now, as the season goes on, and take far more than half of my fish from the tailouts in July and August.

The body of a small mountain pool is often no more than three or four feet deep. But it is a lot deeper than the water around it. And it often butts against a cliff or steep bank, giving it shade, making it a lot darker. In fact, darkness is to me the definition of some of the best water in the smallest streams. It took years for me to learn to cast a dry fly to these almost-still waters, then to let it sit while I thought about something else. For some reason a fly can sit unattended for a minute or two, in full sight of whatever fish might be down there. Then suddenly something stimulates the fish—anger or hunger or impatience—and the pool is rent.

I still fish the heads of the pools, too, just as I always did. And I take lots of fish there, drifting a dry on the frothed water itself, or just to the sides of it, down the seams where fast water and slow are sewn together. But now I fish all the parts of a pool: the tailout, body, and head. I take nearly equal numbers of fish from all three.

The tackle for this kind of fishing should suit the size of the streams. But this does not mean going down to the very lightest number-two or -three lines. Those are for tiny flies, and small-stream trout usually see larger grub. I prefer a seven-foot rod for a number-four line, though a seven-and-a-half-footer for a number-five would be just as effective. For me, the primary criteria for the rod are quickness and accuracy. I hate a weepy rod when making short, tight casts with a dry fly. A soft rod that does not direct the fly exactly where I want it frustrates me when I'm trying to make thirty-foot shots into something smaller than a basketball hoop.

I use double-taper lines. If your rod is properly balanced with a weight-forward taper, it doesn't make much difference, since the casts will be so short. The leader should be about the length of the rod, with a two-foot tippet added in midsummer, when the water gets low. I use two- or three-pound tippets. They are a little light for bushy dry flies, but with short leaders they turn them over well enough, and anything stouter would seem a shame matched against ten- to twelve-inch trout.

The flies are usually attractor drys. The Royal Wulff is excellent. For several seasons I used nothing else. I could see it because of its white wings; trout could see it because of its bulk. They took it eagerly. They still do. At the advent of the Elk Hair Caddis, I switched to it and used it almost exclusively for the next few years. Only in recent seasons have I added a few new flies to the single fly box I carry on my home creeks.

The first added pattern is a Beetlebug, as tied by Robert Borden, creator of Hare Line Dubbing. His Beetlebug is tied with a fluorescent red fur body, white calf-body hairwings, moose-hair tails, and coachman brown hackle. It looks a lot like the Royal Wulff. But it must look like something better to eat to small-stream trout. For some reason they take it more often, and more eagerly, at least on my streams.

The other fly I have added is a soft-hackled wet fly, the Partridge and Yellow. I am still experimenting with wets on small streams. I have been delving into the old books: Stewart's 1857 *The Practical Angler*, and Cutcliffe's 1863 *Trout Fishing on Rapid Streams*. Their advice applies to today's fishing a lot better than some of today's advice. And it is a lot less complicated. They said to fish wets upstream when the sun was on the water. It works.

Successful tactics on small streams have three parts. First, you should fish the tailout, body, and head of each pool or short run as you come to it. But if you fish for a couple of hours and discover trout are holding in only one of the types of water, then it is fine to concentrate your casting there. Second, you should *stalk the water*, not the fish. Learn to read potential lies, then assume each of them holds a trout. Likely it will. Third, present

Flies for fishing mountain creeks.

your fly so it lands on the water rather abruptly, as if it were a natural insect surprised to find itself there. Fish will be surprised, too, and move to take it before they have time to decide it's the wrong kind of groceries.

A full day on a mountain creek has a specific shape for me. It starts out in the morning with a #12 Beetlebug. Light is a bit subdued before the sun rises to where it shines down into the canyon and through the trees to strike the water. The white wings of the bug are visible, easy to follow against the darkness of the stream. And trout rise willingly to the dark-bodied fly, while at the end of the day, for some reason that I cannot explain, they don't move so much for the light Elk Hair Caddis.

When the sun gets up in its arc, around ten or eleven o'clock, so that it strikes straight down, I switch to a soft-hackled wet fly, the

Partridge and Yellow in #10 or #12. Trout are reluctant to rise to anything bright in this light. They are slightly hesitant to rise at all. But they move dashingly for anything that comes to them in the drift, beneath the surface. At times, in bright light, I take two or three times as many trout on wets as I can draw up to drys.

This kind of fishing takes intense concentration. Nothing will put you in closer touch with a tiny stream than fishing it with upstream wet flies. You have to watch for any twitch of your line tip or the subdued wink under water that tells you a trout has taken your fly. After you've fished this way for a season or so, you begin to take fish without any knowledge of what made you raise the rod to set the hook.

When the sun has tipped over the canyon in the afternoon and no longer strikes the water directly, I find that lots of caddis, mayfly spinners, and small stoneflies come out and begin the dances that will last until evening. I switch then to the #14 Elk Hair Caddis that at one time was the only fly I used on tiny streams. As light fades, trout take it more and more willingly.

The three-part approach to the water, fishing the tailout, body, and head of every run and pool, has added a lot of fish to my small-stream fishing. The three-part approach to the day, changing flies with the waxing and waning of the light of the sun, has changed the hours when I expected only an occasional fish into hours when I expect a fish from almost every holding lie.

My tackle and tactics are under constant refinement. I discover something different every time out. If I fished your mountain streams, I might find that new flies, and new tactics, would work better there.

Creeks are clinics when it comes to the study of finding fish and of discovering what works to take them. They are often demeaned by those who fish larger waters for larger trout. But they can give you lots of lessons that prepare you for those other fishing situations.

12

Classic Freestone Trout Streams

Medium-sized trout streams are what most of us fish most of the time. They are classic water, of a personable size. They are comfortable to wade; they are about a long fly cast across. They are the kind of water that a lot of this book has been about, so they will get just a minor review here.

Classic trout streams are freestone, arising from run-off sources. They have all the water types discussed in the chapters of this book. They display the standard riffle-to-run-to-pool structure. They get knocked out of shape by rains in winter, by run-off and melt-water in spring. They are perfect for fishing after the freshets subside in June and July. They are subject to low flows and often have temperature and oxygen problems in August and early September. They are refreshed again for a few weeks in fall, and most people turn their backs on good fishing after the first early frosts of October.

These streams are deep enough in most of their stretches, for most of the year, to make it profitable to keep in mind the three levels of the water: bottom, mid-depths, and top. Each type of

Classic trout stream with a riffle-run-pool structure.

water, and each level within each type, will be important according to where and when trout hold there, and whether they rest or feed actively when they are there.

The structure of the stream depends on the geography through which it flows. Its gradient reflects the steepness of the country around it, and its streambed is determined largely by its gradient. The closer it is to its mountain-creek sources the more bouldered its course will be, and the closer its fishing will be to the plunge-pool type described in the last chapter.

As a stream grows and approaches downstream maturity, it flattens. Its course tends to meander more, its bottom is composed of finer and finer material, first predominantly rock, then cobble, then pebbles, and finally sand. We hope the stream gets to be a large trout river before its bottom becomes largely sand and silt, but most don't.

The water types that are most important in a given stream will also depend on its gradient. In average trout streams, all the water types are present and most are important. Choppy riffles provide lots of feed. Three- to four-foot-deep runs have lots of holding water. The three parts of pools can all be important: the head, body, and tailout. Rapids and cascades will have a few pockets of fine holding water. The banks of a classic trout stream are usually too shallow, the water too slow along them, or lacking in sufficient features, to hold trout. But there will be some bank water that the observant angler, who knows what kind of water meets the three needs of the trout, will find not only very productive, but also rarely fished.

Productive flats are usually absent from classic freestone trout streams. Aquatic vegetation rarely has a chance to take root, leaving the flats barren of protection for feeding trout.

The needs of trout in medium-sized streams are met in almost all of the ways that have been discussed throughout the length of this book. These streams are large enough to offer shelter from currents in almost all of the water types. If they are very small, the riffles might be too thin to have more than half a dozen holding lies for trout half a foot long. But more and larger trout will hold in runs or pools nearby, and move up to the riffles to feed when insects are active enough to make it worth the risk and the loss of energy it takes to feed in shallow, brisk water.

Protection from predators is a factor that trout respond to in classic streams. There will be empty water that might hold fish if only it met this need, or had a bomb shelter nearby to which the fish could bolt when pressed by bird, otter, or man. In larger freestone streams, most water types offer sufficient protection until late in the summer, when the water is low. Fish hold throughout the stream, then move into the most sheltered areas as the water gets lower. Being able to read the water as it drops, and realizing that the water no longer meets one of the needs of the trout, will give you a clue to their movements as the season progresses.

The movement of trout from one water type to the next is perhaps greatest in these kinds of streams, where all the water types might be within a hundred feet of each other. At times you will find all of the trout, or at least all of the *willing* trout, in one type of water. When this happens you can hop from riffle to riffle, or run to run, leaving others to fish all of the water, in which case they will be spending most of it on water that is not productive at that time. But what works one day might not work the next. The fish might move – they will move – leaving you to fish the unproductive water if you keep your eyes and mind closed.

The need for food is met in classic freestone streams by all of the variety that both the aquatic and terrestrial worlds have to offer. But there is a larger chance that one species of insect will be dominant at one time and that you will have to fish a fly that resembles it at least reasonably in order to take trout.

As in mountain creeks, the importance of terrestrials is related to the size of the stream. On large streams, their importance diminishes except at times when large numbers of a single insect fall to the water in a limited location, usually along a bank. The kinds of terrestrials that are important vary with the type of vegetation along the banks. In grasslands, grasshoppers are most important. In forest lands beetles, ants, termites, inchworms, and leafhoppers get the most nods from trout. When a specific terrestrial is dominant, a match for it will help you fool fish.

Trout are occupied most of the time in freestone streams with the need to find food. They hold their stations, winnowing insects from the drift at all levels. If a hatch comes off they move to a location that enables them to feed more successfully on it. Sometimes they merely drift a little higher on their stations; at other times they hold just under the surface or move off their territory entirely to feed in some other type of water.

Freestone streams have holding lies, feeding lies, and prime lies. When trout rest on a holding lie, they are usually, but not always, willing to feed. When on feeding lies, they are usually feeding on something specific and want something that looks a little like it presented at the right level in the water with the right motion to represent the natural insect's behavior. When trout are on prime lies, they will be holding a station and feeding on whatever the current brings. They will usually move for a properly presented fly if they don't have to go far to get it.

Tackle on freestone streams should be about what we consider to be average, or standard, gear. Rods should be eight to nine feet long, balanced to cast number-five and -six lines. Most people today use weight-forward lines for the slight advantage they give in casting distance. I feel that the streams have not grown in the last few years; I still prefer double-tapers for the control they give me over the fly once it is in or on the water. Two of my favorite outfits are an eight-foot rod for a five-weight line, and an eight-and-one-half-foot rod for a six-weight. Most days I reach for one or the other, depending on the size of the stream to be fished that day.

Most of the time my leader for classic stream fishing is hand-tied, ten feet long. I use it at that length, or shorten it a bit, if the situation calls for the deep nymph. I leave it at ten feet for mid-depth nymph and wet-fly fishing. When I switch to the dry fly on the surface, I add a couple of feet of appropriate tippet and have a twelve-foot leader. This seems adequate on even the smoothest of freestone-type water. If a specific hatch calls for a tiny fly, I add six-inch sections of progressively finer leader to the ten-foot basic leader until I arrive at the right tippet size to balance the fly. The tippet, again, is usually about two feet long.

When a hatch is happening, I try to discover the stage the fish are taking, and the level at which they are taking it. Then I try an impressionistic pattern that looks a bit like it. This might be a Zug Bug or Gold-Ribbed Hare's Ear on the bottom, a traditional wet fly or a soft-hackled wet at mid-depths, a Catskill dry or an Elk Hair Caddis on the surface. Only if these fail do I begin the process of collecting and precisely matching the hatch. This simple approach solves most of the problems before they get complicated. But complicated problems are some of the most enjoyable reasons to fly fish; you want to be able to solve them when you have to.

Effective presentations on freestone streams are usually upstream. Most holding water and prime lies can be fished this way: moving up, fishing the water, probing the specific lies as you come to them. Fish each of the water types, and each of the levels, according to the best way to take trout from it. This generally requires a bit of tackle changing, from dry to wet or nymph and back to dry again. But the slight extra effort is worth it, and will probably cease as soon as you discover that there is one level at which the fish prefer to feed.

On a typical day astream I start fishing upstream, planning to cover quite a bit of water to make sure I see all the water types. If I am boating, of course, the float gives me a view of all that the water offers. Either way, make sure you correct the common problem of going to the stream and remaining rooted to one spot all day. I don't know how many times I've seen folks fishing fruitlessly in one water type, far more gracefully than I could, while I was able to flail away and take some trout because trout were more active just a little distance up or down the stream.

On my typical day, I'll start with a dry fly, likely an Elk Hair Caddis in size twelve or size fourteen. I'll fish it first in the corner of a riffle or run, where its entry leaves a slight eddy off to the side. This is one of the first places I always look for fish. If it fails to produce, I'll try a riffle or a run. If no fish come to the dry, then I'll try a wet fly or unweighted nymph for a while in the same kind of water.

If no trout come to either the dry fly or the shallow wet or nymph, then I'll switch to fishing a nymph down on the bottom. To be honest, in my own fishing I usually catch enough fish on drys or shallow wets to keep me happy. I prefer to fish with the uncomplicated gear. But I should be more willing to switch. I'm not as good at nymph fishing as I should be; when I fish with someone who is an expert at it he will usually wipe my eye. And he usually takes bigger fish.

Always keep an eye out for rising trout. If you find them, fish for them. I have fished time after time with people who have passed up rising fish, saying, "Let's go on upstream. There's better water up there." Half the time there is better water up there, but no trout rising in it.

Never pass up a rising trout is my motto. Of course, it doesn't have to be yours.

13

Tackle and Tactics
for Large Rivers

The special attractions of large rivers are more in their fish, less in the rivers themselves. Although some are among the most beautiful streams in the world, most are known more for the chance to take a trophy trout than they are for the beauty of the surroundings in which the trout is taken.

Large trout rivers are the hardest water to read. Their holding lies are extensive; all of their features are out of proportion. Runs are long, wide, and deep enough to conceal the bottom. Pools are broad, inscrutable. Almost all of the features that create specific lies are down deep, hidden from sight. On large water, you read a piece of the river to calculate its potential for holding trout, then you fish the water with a disciplined casting pattern, knowing that your fly will explore until it finds a specific holding lie and entices a trout.

As with all stream types, the type of terrain determines the gradient of a large river. Some are at the lower ends of watersheds, in broad valleys. Erosion has had some chance to flatten out the streambed and to grind down the rocks. Rapids and

Classic run on a big western river.

cascades are rare. The bottom is usually composed of fairly fine material. Most big rivers suffer some effects from timber harvesting, overgrazing, or irrigation draw-down. The combination of natural erosion and manmade problems nearly always causes silting to be a factor on large rivers.

But other big rivers are found in mountainous regions and have more of the features of mid-sized streams, though the features are greatly enlarged. The upper Madison River, as an example, is called a fifty-mile riffle. It has lots of boulders and pocket water. Its banks are excellent. There are few pools.

The Yellowstone has a classic structure, but its riffles carry so much water they verge on rapids. Its runs are sometimes two hundred yards long. The Big Hole River has pools you can't cast far enough to cover with a fly. But it is often described as the world's classic trout stream. It's all the same stream structure, but the size of the stream is relative.

Big rivers have all the various water types that other streams have. They are the same, but much larger. Riffles are less frequent, but when you find one it is usually a giant, and so productive that hundreds of trout live on its bounty. As with all streams, if the riffle is deep and slow enough, and has sufficient interruptions in its current, it will hold trout. If trout cannot hold in the riffle, they will be found holding in the nearest comfortable water below it, living on the richness delivered down from it.

Runs are what we think of when we think of holding water in big rivers. They usually have shallow gravel bars on one side, are wide and so deep in the center and toward the other side that the structure of the bottom seldom reflects up to the surface. The best holding water is usually in the deepest part of the run, which is toward the outside if the run is located on a bend in the river.

Runs that are productive in big rivers have a current that is definable, if not strong. They are usually deeper than three or four feet. In shallower runs you can expect to find the same kind of trout you would find at the same depth in smaller streams. In runs typical of larger rivers, the depth will be from four to eight feet, and the fish will be bigger than what you would expect to find in a typical trout stream.

Pools in big rivers are broad, deep, difficult to fish, and have the potential for producing the biggest trout. They are almost a study in themselves, like small lakes. And like small lakes, they hold their trout in the deepest water most of the time but send them out to feed in the shallows on occasion, usually at dusk.

Flats are not common features of big water. But some rivers have them, and rivers with spring-creek origins, such as the famous Henry's Fork of the Snake, are known for their broad, shallow, and almost still flats.

Pocket water is not a feature we think of when we think of large rivers. Most are too placid. But some rivers carve through canyons and have awesome rapids and cascades. The water is normally unwadable; you can only fish those pockets you can cast to from the banks. If there is any doubt in your mind about this kind of water, keep out of it. The combination of powerful currents, uneven bottoms, and the slipperiness that is typical of a big river's rocks make them excellent places to drown, which is one of the worst things you can accomplish during a day of fishing.

Good bank water is common on large rivers. Many reaches are deep, with strong currents rubbing right against the shore. This becomes especially important water during the migration of giant salmon fly nymphs, when trout wait along the banks for the emerging nymphs, and during the hatch itself, when the clumsy adults creep around in riverside grasses and willows, falling into the water at irregular intervals that keep big trout waiting, ready to rush upward.

Many big rivers have sections with all the aspects of small-to-medium trout streams. These are broken up by braided channels or side channels that split the river into more manageable – and more readable – portions. These streams within large rivers should be treated exactly as they appear. They are some of the easiest water to read on a large river and they provide some of its best fishing. But the fish are usually the size found on streams, not big rivers, and the largest trout are usually caught elsewhere in the river.

When reading big water to locate big fish, look for the same things you look for on smaller water: places where the water meets the three needs of the trout.

There are lots of lies where trout can find shelter from strong currents in large rivers. But you can seldom see them. They are deep in the darkness of a pool or so far down in a run that they are not visible from the surface. Of course, when you can see them you should fish them. But most of the time, you will have to identify likely holding water, then fish all of it to get your fly into the specific holding lies.

Protection from predators is almost universal in large rivers, except when they come out to feed on flats, or move up high in the water of runs, or back down into the tailouts of pools. Then they are just as exposed to predation as if they were in the thinnest of mountain streams, and they will be just as wary.

The primary sources of food in large rivers are the same aquatic and terrestrial insects that make up the diet in other streams. The variety of species is likely to be a bit narrower, and in large areas of similar water type, for example a long, deep run, a single species is more likely to be dominant. If fish are found feeding on a hatch, they will be just as selective as they are in any other stream type. You will have to determine what stage of the insect they take and where they take it – the bottom, mid-depths, or top. Then you will have to select a specific dressing that matches the insect and present it in the manner of the natural's movement.

Terrestrials are less likely to be an important food source on a consistent basis to all of the trout in a big river because the water along the banks is a much smaller proportion of the total width of the river. But terrestrial insects are extremely important to trout along the banks, and the banks are about the most impor-tant bit of water to the boating angler.

Larger organisms become more important in the deep water of larger rivers. Baitfish and crayfish, trout fry and sculpins, leeches and landborne beasts like mice can all get into the wrong water and get chased down by large predatory fish. Most folks fishing large rivers hope for large fish. One way to increase that hope is to fish with flies that represent the largest bites a fish is likely to see.

The occupation of trout in a big river is the same as for their friends in smaller streams. They spend most of their time on stations, taking feed from territories. The size of the territory is likely to be much larger, and the features that cause suitable territories are likely to be less abundant, more scattered. Fish will, therefore, be spread out in big rivers.

Most of a large trout's time is spent holding, resting, waiting for the right time to chase something worth chasing. But a small or average trout will feed on the drift that comes to it. At times, when feed is abundant and concentrated in a certain water type, trout will move off their stations and concentrate at the food source. But the larger the trout, the larger the amount of food it takes to entice it to move. The largest trout, over four or five pounds, are caught where they live and seldom anywhere else. You've usually got to go to them, or at least get your fly to them, right down in their territories.

Going to them takes special gear, and calls for special tactics. Rods for fishing big rivers should be long, nine feet or longer, and stout enough to propel eight-, nine-, or even ten-weight lines. Most of your fishing should be done along the bottom. Most of the water you fish can be probed with combination floating/ sinking lines. A ten-foot wet-tip might get a fly to the bottom in runs three to four feet deep. But for typical big-river runs, a wet-head line, with thirty feet of fast-sinking line and the rest of the running line floating, will get it down faster and keep it down better.

Many people who fish the largest rivers, such as the Yellowstone downstream from the park, use shooting-head systems. These have a thirty-foot section of fast-sinking line backed by one hundred feet of Cobra or Amnesia monofilament. One hundred fifty to two hundred yards of Dacron or nylon backing fills the rest of the reel. In order to make the system work over a wide range of water conditions without carrying a battery of reels, just carry a series of shooting heads in various sink rates, all balanced to the same rod. Loops at the end of the monofilament and the shooting lines let you switch in a hurry without changing spools on the reel.

Lines to carry would include a floater or an intermediate, a slow sinker, a fast sinker, and a super-fast-sinking head. The line to choose in a given situation would be the one that gets your fly to the bottom in that type of water, which calls for calculating the combined factors of its speed and its depth.

The leader should be kept short, three to five feet. It should be heavy enough to withstand a brutal strike or to play a large fish in a strong current. That means a tippet in the eight- to twelve-pound-test category. You will have to tie your own leaders; they are not available in these lengths and with this kind of stoutness. But you can get by with a level leader, or one with a heavy butt, a single and short transitional mid-section, and a tippet of the strength you desire. It doesn't take much to tie a leader for this type of fishing. You can do it on the stream in a couple of minutes if you carry the three or four leader spools you need.

Flies for the banks and for the shallows should be typical of what you would use in that type of water on smaller streams. If you need to match the hatch, your gear should balance the flies you will use; don't try to fish size-twenty drys with the shooting systems I described above. They are for fishing big water with big flies, for big fish.

Most big-water fishing calls for either large and heavily

weighted nymphs, or streamers. Nymphs should be Bitch Creeks, Montana Nymphs, Yuk Bugs, or similar ugly creations. They should be tied on #4 or #6 4XL hooks. The weight on them, as they are tied by commercial tiers, is the same diameter as the hook shank and extends in tight wraps the length of it. That's a lot of lead. Don't try to toss it with your five-weight.

Streamers should be of the sculpin variety. Spuddlers and Muddlers are always popular, although there are a lot more complicated and more realistic dressings available. They should be tied on hooks from #6 to 2/0. Number two is a good size until you feel you could do better with something larger. That's plenty of fly to toss with an eight- or nine-weight rod.

Other popular streamers include Marabou Muddlers and Spruce Flies, Matukas and Woolly Buggers. The Olive and Black Woolly Bugger is catching as many big trout as any other fly these days, and it is very simple to tie. It consists merely of a marabou tail, chenille body, and hackle palmered the length of the body. It is used in #6 to #2, with the hook shank under the chenille wrapped heavily with lead wire. When the marabou tail of a Woolly Bugger gets to waving in the current, either along the bank or down on the bottom, it looks like something with its afterburners on, swimming like hell to escape a trout. Big trout seem naturally to want to whack it.

Presentation on big water, with these big weighted flies, calls for casts that are slightly upstream, to give the fly a substantial portion of its drift just to get down to the bottom. Let the line tighten against it, then swing the fly around until it is straight downstream. You might want to pulse your rod tip, making the fly appear to swim around in the current along the bottom.

It is common to cast as far as you can when fishing big water. It is probably more productive to keep the casts to a reasonable distance, say fifty to sixty feet, and have more control over the drift of the fly and the setting of the hook. But where the water warrants it, wade deep, cast long, and try to cover the deepest water. If you can cast farther than most people can, you might be able to show your fly to a fish that has never seen one. But a lot of people who fish big rivers with balanced gear can cast beyond one hundred feet, sometimes into the wall of a wind.

It can be worth the cost of the assemblage of correct gear to

Ted Richings with a nice brown taken from the Bighorn River.

make these long casts, and the time it takes to learn to use it correctly. A trout that has never seen a fly might be a big one, especially on a big river.

Be patient on large rivers. You won't catch as many fish. But your chance of catching the biggest trout of your life is greater here than it is on any other moving water.

14

Meadow Streams and Spring Creeks

Meadow streams and spring creeks are about the most beautiful places trout abound. Their peaceful flows meander through pastoral landscapes, wilderness meadows, or jack-pine forests. Their water is clear and bright, with tails of lush green vegetation waving gracefully in soft currents. Aquatic insect hatches are prolific, and even they seem to include the most beautiful of their kind: the early-spring Little Olives, the midseason Sulphurs, and the dancing and dainty caddis of August and September.

Trout in meadow streams are doubly difficult because they are wary in the first place and get lots of opportunity to examine your fly and its presentation in the second place. They are wary because the clear, slow water exposes them to natural predation, and their fine environment attracts the most deceitful and unnatural predator of all: man and his fly rod. The same glassy water gives them ample time to inspect what you offer them. Rejection is far more common than acceptance.

Meadow-stream trout are the most selective of all. Meadow streams have gentle gradients. If the land were steep, the streams would be freestone. Though we tend to think of them as one type of water, in fact most meadow streams have freestone stretches. The Metolius in Oregon is a prime example. It originates in springheads. It flows for miles through ponderosa flats: meandering, gentle, with a stable bed, trailing weeds, and undercut banks. Then of a sudden it tips down and carves through a canyon in volcanic rock. It is brutal in this two-mile reach, with a few pieces of pocket water that can be timidly touched from shore. Few fishermen dare it.

Below the canyon the Metolius gentles out again, into several miles of typical meadow stream. It gathers water from more springs, and grows to where you can wade only a few of its shallower flats. Finally it tips down again and makes its final miles to the Deschutes River in a rush of white water. Again, there is little here but a few pockets that can be fished with difficulty from shore.

Many meadow streams originate as spring creeks, for the simple reason that it requires a stable flow to create the conditions that we usually think of as defining meadow streams. But even the most rambunctious freestone streams mellow out in places where the gradient is not steep. In these reaches they take on some of the characteristics of meadow streams. But not all of them. Without stable flows the stream will alternately erode its

Silver Creek in Idaho is a classic spring creek.

banks, then retreat within them. And it will not harbor attached algae or rooted vegetation if it is subject to winter and spring scour.

For the purposes of this book, a meadow stream is any stream with a gentle gradient, with a slow current that primarily takes the form of flats and slick-surfaced runs, and with stable banks and at least a minor amount of aquatic vegetation.

The most important water types in meadow streams are flats, smooth runs, and the water along the banks of both. Water types that are not characteristic of meadow streams include riffles, broken runs, pools, and pocket water. But there will be stretches of these kinds of water along the course of any stream. When you encounter them they can be important water, and you should fish them carefully according to their kind.

Riffles or broken runs interspersed with more typical meadow-stream water can attract trout from long distances. If a short reach of rougher water contains the only safe holding lies in a couple hundred feet of stream, trout will take up territories there and move out to the flats only when a hatch is on. Fishing the broken water of a meadow stream can be a brilliant strategy. The fishing is somewhat easier, but that is not the main reason it's smart to seek it out. The primary reason is that it extends your fishing into the many hours when trout are not actively feeding on flat water. The secondary reason is that some of the largest trout on a flat drop down into other water types as they get larger and need bigger and safer territories.

But flats are the kind of water we associate with spring creeks and meadow streams, and it is best to focus on them and notice how they meet the needs of trout. The need for shelter is met rather gracefully, since the currents are not strong enough to need much breaking. Weed beds give trout all the shelter they need; shallow trenches in the bottom also serve to break the bottom. Trenches are found most commonly in meadow streams that flow through volcanic country.

The need for protection from predators is met only when the trout are on their holding lies, which they will choose for the protection they give. But we normally fish meadow streams for trout that are feeding, not holding in protected lies. When they are feeding, their only defense is a superb wariness. They flee on flats at the slightest sign of a bird or line passing overhead, or of a man creeping into their window on the world. The value of a flat as a feeding lie will be enhanced considerably by the presence of a nearby bomb shelter, where trout can escape into perfect protection.

Foods on meadow-stream flats are generally prolific. The aquatic insects tend toward a few dominant species, with representatives among the mayflies, caddisflies, and midges most common.

Terrestrial insects have total importance in proportion to the width of any meadow stream, but it has recently been discovered that all streams of this type have banks, no matter how wide the water, and that the water along the banks is important even if it is a small proportion of the total water. Because of their relatively constant flow, meadow streams tend to be almost as deep at the banks as they are over the rest of their width. But the cover is better at the edge, where grasses and willows overhang the water and offer protection. Wherever there is a fair current along the banks, trout will hold, and terrestrials will be a major part of their diet.

Small crustaceans reach their greatest importance in spring-creek flats. A combination of factors comes together to make this true: stable flows encourage weed growth, and so do mineral-rich spring waters. Crustaceans love to paddle about in weeds, and they thrive in calcium-rich water. Scuds are the most abundant and the most interesting to trout. Cress bugs, also called water sow bugs, are not as widespread, but they are important on some Pennsylvania limestone waters.

Trout tend to be either feeding visibly or not feeding at all on meadow streams. When they are feeding that is their sole occupation; when they are not feeding they usually rest in holding lies. They probably feed there as willingly as any trout on its station, observing the drift. But a holding lie in a weed bed is a tough place to present a fly so that a resting trout can get a fair look at it. Sometimes in the weeds there are trenches wide enough to stalk and to drift a nymph down. Most of the time it's a tough proposition, and most meadow-stream anglers prefer to wait for signs of active feeding.

When feed is available, trout will move out to take it at all levels. And they will be extremely wary when they do, their wariness increasing as they feed nearer and nearer the surface.

Tackle and tactics for meadow streams are a rehash of those discussed in Chapter 8. Rods should be long and light. Lines in the four- and five-weight class work best, though there is a movement toward even lighter two- and three-weight lines. These are not very useful when the wind comes up, though, and the rods that cast them should be considered specialty rods. Dry lines are sufficient to fish most meadow-stream situations. If you want to fish deep, use weight on the leader and it will get to the bottom if you cast a bit upstream and give the fly time to sink.

Leaders should be twelve to fifteen feet long, and tapered down to tippets that balance the flies to be cast. On such smooth water long tippets are a help: the difference between an eighteen-inch tippet and a three-foot tippet is often a lot of fish that come to the fly. A long tippet is more relaxed on the water and gives the fly a more natural float.

You almost need to carry special fly boxes to fish meadow streams. The hatches are specific and you should be able to match them with reasonable accuracy. It helps to carry flies for all the levels at which trout feed.

Flies for the bottom should be small nymph dressings, based on the larvae of caddis and the nymphs of mayflies. Weight will help get them down, but too much weight will sink them too quickly in gentle water. Use just a few turns of lead under the body of the fly and add lead to the leader if you are not getting down.

For fishing at mid-depths, unweighted nymphs, traditional wet flies, and soft-hackled wets all work well. The best policy is to try to collect a sample of what the fish are taking, then select a dressing that resembles it and has a lifelike action in the water.

Weeded meadow streams and spring creeks are rich in a specific problem: the emerger stage of the aquatic insect. Small mayflies and even smaller midges run into the same problem: they bump up against the surface film, and there they're stuck. It's quite a barrier to penetrate if you are a tiny insect. Sometimes hundreds of individuals hang just below the surface; they are the easiest of pickings for trout, and the result is selective feeding that will drive you mad if you try to fish with dry flies. Nymph

Rick Hafele on a typical meadow stream with a few features and lots of good bank water.

dressings with a ball of fur or polypropylene yarn on the back will hang in the surface, just like a natural, and at times can change your luck amazingly.

When trout do feed on the surface, it will be necessary to fish for them with flies that match the naturals they are taking. The smoother the water, the more heavily it is fished, the more accurately you will need to copy the natural. But always recall that presentation is at least as important as fly pattern on this type of water.

On meadow streams you read the fish, not the water, and calculate your presentation based on what they are doing. First you must find the stage of the insect being fed upon and determine at what level the trout are taking it. Then present your fly in a way that suits the actions of the natural.

Fishing deep, with nymphs, calls for upstream presentations.

An indicator will help in this kind of fishing at times, but it can also be an awkward object that frightens the fish when it lands on the water. You will often be better off to eliminate the indicator, grease your leader to a point about twice the depth of the water, and then concentrate raptly on the end of your line. The line tip, in effect, becomes your indicator.

Fishing at mid-depths in smooth water usually calls for across-stream casts, stalking the fish so that you can bring the fly down to them without the leader going over them first. Another excellent tactic is to get into position up and across from a rising fish. Then cast just beyond it and a couple of feet upstream. Let the fly swing down and across in front of the fish and you will often feel a satisfying but sullen pull. Drop the rod tip if you can muster the discipline, and the hook will set itself into the corner of the trout's mouth. This is the same method used in greased-line Atlantic salmon and summer steelhead fishing, and it takes a lot of practice to learn it right.

Emerger patterns should be fished downstream, with slack-line casts, from an angle of about forty-five to sixty degrees. This puts the fly over the fish ahead of line and leader, and is the best way to fool trout that are angler-shy. Upstream presentations work on rumpled water, but not when the surface is smooth.

Dry-fly tactics are the same as emerger tactics, with the downstream cast most effective. Wobble your rod as the line straightens out on the forward cast, and it will land on the water in a series of S-turns. As the line straightens on the water the slack will pull out and the fly will drift without drag down to the fish.

Whatever kind of fly you use, and whatever level you fish, be patient. It takes a lot of casts before the fly arrives at the right moment, in the right way, in front of the right trout. When it does, the take will be subtle. Raise the rod softly to set the hook, then hold on when the trout bores for the weeds.

Meadow streams offer a special kind of fishing, with the rewards not the size or the number of fish caught, but the satisfaction of knowing that you beat them at the best of their games.

15

Trout of the Tailwaters

The attraction of tailwater fisheries is simple: they have an abundance of trout, sometimes including extremely large ones. Tailwater flows are stable, not subject to winter spate, spring runoff, and summer lows. The temperature of the water, coming as it does from the depths of a reservoir, remains relatively constant. This stability of both flow and water temperature keeps the best tailwaters within the ideal range for insect numbers and trout growth all year round. That is why the fish have the potential to grow so large: there is food available, and they keep eating it, right through the year.

The river below a dam is enriched, in many cases, by planktonic growth in the reservoir above the dam. Plankton does not form in fast water; it grows only in the backwaters and along the still edges of streams. But put a dam on a stream's course and plankton thrives in the lake above it. This richness is delivered to the stream below via the dam's outflow. Populations of insects that can use it as a food source explode to take advantage of the sudden influx of groceries.

Roger Lattimer and Mike Schollmeyer fishing the Bighorn tailwater just below the dam.

The most famous tailwaters are features of arid western country. The San Juan River in New Mexico and the Bighorn River in Montana are examples. But there are excellent tailwaters in the Ozarks, others that are less famous throughout the South, and many smaller tailwaters all over this country and Canada that offer excellent fishing.

Many tailwaters have dangerous fluctuations in their water flows. When the tailwater is formed by a power dam, the release of water is timed to high demand for electricity in the area served by the dam. These types of tailwaters can offer excellent fishing, but they can also be dangerous to fish. If you are wading deep and the water starts to rise, by the time you notice it you might be cut off from shore. If you make plans to fish a tailwater, be sure to find out what sort of fluctuations it has, find out if it has a warning signal before the water rises, and be extremely cautious in your wading no matter what the situation.

Most good tailwaters are formed by dams placed for either irrigation or flood control. These are subject to seasonal adjustments in flow, but seldom to daily changes. They are much more trustworthy, though they are still worth some caution.

The typical river that results in a great tailwater fishery is a large system toward the warm-water end of its flowage. Years of silting have destroyed the bottom; seasons of high temperatures have changed the fish life from trout to species that thrive in temperature and oxygen regimes that our favorite fish could not survive. When such a river is dammed, there are two overriding results: first, the reservoir serves as a settling basin for silt; second, the depth of the water cools it, and the water released is just right for trout.

The result is a river below the dam that has aspects of both freestone and meadow streams. The bottom structure is that of a freestone stream, though it remains the type found in a typical lower-river system, with pebble and sand bottoms more common than boulder and stone. But if the river had a bouldered bottom before the dam was built, it will have the same after the dam. And it does get washed by newly clean flows, so a lot of the silt is removed.

Because the flow is stable, not subject to scour, rooted vegetation and attached algae both get a chance to take hold, giving a tailwater river many of the aspects of a spring creek. This is perhaps the most important aspect: the richness of the vegetation harbors food for trout.

All water types are important on tailwater fisheries. Riffles tend to be large, as they are on large rivers. But the stability allows for a richer vegetative growth, and riffles can be extremely rich in insect life. If there are places for trout to hold in them, they will be among the best places to fish. But they will not offer the largest fish in a tailwater because both the size of the bites and the size of the territories are too small to attract the largest trout.

Runs can be very rich in tailwater streams. They offer the protective holding lies of freestone streams but have the added benefit of vegetation and more insect life. A freestone run is not often as rich as a riffle; a tailwater run is usually much more productive of both insect and trout life than a freestone riffle.

Pools are prime in tailwaters, though like pools in all big rivers they can be difficult to fish. If you adjust your equipment to suit the size of the water, and if you are patient enough to do the casting required to wait out a big one in big water, your chances here are better than your chances in any other single water type.

Flats are frequent on tailwater streams. Some riffles and runs are tamed to flats by the stable flows below dams. Because of the richness of insect life and the consequent abundant hatches, trout rise freely and often on tailwater flats. This is the kind of water we have come to associate most often with tailwater fishing. But there are many tailwaters on which flats as a water type are no more prevalent and no more important than flats on typical freestone streams, yet it is the few flats that get the most pressure. In such situations smart anglers seek out the runs and pools nearby and find the largest fish holding there unmolested.

Pocket water is found in some parts of most tailwater fisheries. Where it is found it has a slightly higher degree of richness, with attached algae getting a better chance to take hold in sheltered areas within the pocket. As a consequence there is more food, and the pocket is likely to hold larger trout than it would in a typical freestone stream. But the same vegetation that makes pocket water hold larger trout also makes the same pockets a lot harder to reach. Felt soles are not nearly as effective for wading on a bouldered bottom covered with algae as they are in the clean-stoned rapids and cascades of a stream where the algae is washed out each winter.

The banks of tailwater fisheries are apt to be a bit more prosperous than those along a freestone stream without a dam. The constant water level tends to deepen the water next to the banks; instead of the wide gravel bars of normal freestone streams, you get more deep water with a constant and sturdy flow right at the edges. Trout are enticed to hold along the transition line because the aquatic life is rich there, and the chance of terrestrial life makes it even richer.

The needs of trout are met in the various water types in exactly the ways they were described in the earlier chapters on those water types. Trout will seek shelter from currents in the same ways, and in the same kinds of places. They will move into riffles that don't have adequate shelter in response to an abundance of food in the riffle. And they will move back out of the riffles when the food source is gone, seeking shelter in holding lies down below.

The need for protection from predators is also met in the same ways it is met on all freestone and meadow streams. Trout will be comfortable in the runs and pools, extremely wary when feeding on exposed flats. They will choose their lies with protection in mind, and water that looks like it should be full of fish can be empty of them until a hatch is going on. Then it can just boil.

The need for food is met by the same types of insects in the same water type encountered elsewhere. But the list of insect species, due to the constancy of conditions, might be a bit narrower, and the abundance of some species borders on dominance in a given water type. That is why it is very important to be aware of the insects, and to collect some samples, when you fish tailwater fisheries.

You will find mayflies, caddisflies, stoneflies, and midges all abundant in tailwater streams. Net-spinning caddisfly larvae spin nets like a spider's web, and suspend them in the current to capture tiny bits of drift. They thrive in water enriched by plankton, and their populations are awesome in the mileage just downstream from some dams.

Terrestrials are not of any greater importance in tailwaters than they are in freestone streams of similar size. But they are a factor, and fish will feed selectively on them when they are suddenly abundant.

Scuds are extremely important in the weed beds and algal beds below dams. Their populations are often intense; they can be the primary food source for trout throughout the entire winter, when insects are not hatching. And tailwaters are often open to fishing in winter. With their constant flows and stable temperature regimes, they can be excellent fishing all year.

In the largest tailwaters, which hold the largest trout, the largest bites become the most important to you. Crayfish, baitfish, and sculpins are all hunted down by big fish. Leeches can be present, and wherever fish see a few they tend to respond eagerly to imitations of them. If you are after trophy trout, fishing big flies deep in tailwaters is one of the best ways to find one.

Trout spend their time in tailwaters doing the same things they do in other freestone streams. They hold on their stations, feeding on the drift. They are more often tempted into moving up to feed on a hatch, simply because there are more heavy hatches. They are also more apt to feed throughout the year, since the constant water temperatures keep both the aquatic insects and the trout in the range where they are active.

Tackle and tactics for tailwaters usually fall into two categories, though all that has been written in this book about fishing the various water types applies exactly to tailwaters wherever you find the water type described. The two most important types of fishing on tailwaters are big gear on big runs and pools for big fish, and hatch-matching for fish that are also sometimes big, on smooth runs and flats.

Hatch-matching gear, and the tactics employed with it, should be the same as described in Chapter 8. The notes in Chapter 14 also apply to this kind of fishing on tailwaters. Rods should be long and light, lines either double-taper or weight-forward floaters in the four- and five-weight class. Leaders should be twelve to fifteen feet long, tapered to long tippets that balance the size flies being used.

The flies chosen should match the hatch as nearly as you can, and should be appropriate for the level at which you will fish them. Presentations should suit the insect stage trout are taking, and the level at which they are taking it.

Big gear should be the same as that described in Chapter 7 and Chapter 13. The rod should be long, stout, and used to punch out weight-forward lines in eight-, nine-, and even ten-weights. The lines should be wet-heads in various sink rates, or you might want to try the shooting systems so commonly used by those who cast big flies over big water.

The flies should match the biggest bites you expect the trout to see. Woolly Buggers and Muddlers and Marabous are extremely effective, tied on weighted hooks in #6 up to a huge 2/0. Keep the leaders short if you are going to fish down deep, though if you are fishing shallow along the shorelines you might want to use a floating line and a leader a bit shorter than the rod.

You will usually fish this kind of gear in deep runs or big pools. Your tactics should suit that kind of water, with casts that give the fly lots of time to sink and retrieves that bring it scooting back near the bottom.

Tailwaters offer all the water types found on typical freestone streams, with some of the characteristics of spring creeks thrown in. You should use tackle and tactics that suit the water type you

Jim Schollmeyer lands a tailwater trout on the Bighorn River in Montana.

will fish, but remember that the chance of a large trout exists almost anywhere in a tailwater. You should always be prepared to handle a surprise large trout, should one decide to take even your daintiest offering.

Conclusion

We had thirteen miles of the Bighorn River to float before it got dark. But Jim Schollmeyer and I got hung up fishing in the flats just downstream from the dam. Trout rose all around us, tilting up slowly out of weed-bed lies to sip tiny olive mayfly duns that arose from the same source, then sinking down again, out of sight until the next soft rise.

"It's like The Henry's Fork," I called to Jim as I lifted the fly to cast again after another refusal.

"Except the fish are bigger," Jim called back as he set the hook into a fat trout that mistook his #20 Olive Compara-dun for the real thing.

It was our first day on the Bighorn. We recalled lessons learned on lots of other rivers, fishing over lots of rising trout. We presented our flies from upstream, with slack-line casts. Often, but never often enough, everything would gather itself into perfection, and a trout would come gullibly to a fly as if it were a natural. We both did well, though Jim did better.

But it was he who suddenly looked up and said in alarm, "It'll be dark in two hours and we've still got ten miles to go!" We jumped into the johnboat and took turns putting our backs to the oars, urging the boat in a losing race against darkness. As we rowed we watched a lot of river go by that we would rather be fishing. There were choppy riffles, long runs, a few deep pools.

"We've got to get off those flats a little sooner tomorrow," I told Jim, "so we have time to fish some of this other water."

Jim stroked downstream in the dark. "I agree," he answered.

The river turned out to be pretty tame, and we laughed as we splashed through the only rapid marked on our map. "You sure this is it?" Jim kept asking.

"Must be," I answered. "It's just to the left of that island." I pointed. "And there's the bluff above it." I pointed again.

"Wouldn't be a rapid on the Deschutes," Jim said, and we ceased to worry about going down in the dark.

The next day we got hung up in the riffles. They were like the rich broken water that we fish constantly on our Deschutes River floats nearer to home. We fished them the same: upstream casts with Elk Hair and Deer Hair Caddis drys keyed loosely to a natural we noticed working out over the water. Fish rose and popped spray into the air; we had no trouble telling takes.

This time it was I who cried, "It's almost dark and we've got eight miles to go; let's get!" We did, but this time while one rowed the other dapped a dry downstream from the boat. We weren't too worried about getting in before dark; we knew the trail now.

Dapping downstream was a simple matter of reading seams. Wherever currents came together we put the fly where it would ride right down the suture. They didn't all produce, but they were the only features we could see in the failing light. Each of us took about three more trout than we would have caught had we just rowed. Since we didn't stop the boat to play the fish, dapping didn't cost us any extra time.

The next day we parked next to a long run, forced to wait while another party fished a riffle we wanted to try. The run was only about three feet deep, with an even flow for a couple of hundred yards. It reminded me of a run on the Willamette River, and I recalled a time when wet flies had worked wonders for me there. So while we waited I tied on a #14 Light Cahill with swept-back wings and fished slowly down the run with wet-fly swings.

The places where fish rapped the fly were almost predictable; there were slight boils every few feet down the current, marking underwater boulders no larger than typewriters. Whenever the fly swung into position above a boulder I would concentrate and mentally almost coax the fish. It worked; every other boulder put up a fish, some of them around a couple of pounds.

Again the fishing was so good that we got hung up far above camp, and arrived long after dark. On the way down I recalled lessons learned on an earlier Montana float, on a river that writers are obligated not to name. I strung a stout rod, tied on a fat and weighted Woolly Bugger, and punched it out behind the boat when it was Jim's turn to row. I put the fly next to the bank, sometimes bouncing it off rocks and pulling it out of clumps of grass.

I caught only two fish before it was my time to take up the oars. But both weighed more than three pounds.

The Bighorn is one of the hottest trout rivers in the world. It is hard to have bad fishing there. But Jim and I saw anglers from New Jersey and Georgia and Texas, some having excellent fishing, others having fishing no better than they might have had at home. Those who did well arrowed right to the best water, and fished each water type with a method that suited it. Those who didn't do well wandered down the river, fishing it all with the same method, or even worse, stopping in one spot and fishing it for the rest of the day without ever moving.

You can learn what to look for on a river by reading books. They will tell you about the needs of trout and how the water moves to fill them. But the ultimate lessons in reading water are learned on streams, the instructors the trout.

And every lesson you learn, no matter where you learn it, transfers to all other rivers, no matter where you fish.

Bibliography

Bergman, Ray. *Trout*. New York: Alfred A. Knopf, 1938.

Brooks, Charles. *The Trout and the Stream*. New York: Crown Publishers, 1974.

Cutcliffe, H. C. *Trout Fishing on Rapid Streams*. South Molton: 1863.

Hafele, Rick. *Anatomy of a Trout Stream*. St. Paul: 3M Scientific Anglers, 1986 (video and companion book).

————. *Aquatic Insects and Their Imitations*. Boulder: Johnson Books, 1987.

Hafele, Rick, and Dave Hughes. *The Complete Book of Western Hatches*. Portland: Frank Amato Publications, 1981.

Hughes, Dave. *Handbook of Hatches*. Harrisburg: Stackpole Books, 1987.

Hynes, H. B. N. *The Ecology of Running Waters*. Toronto: University of Toronto Press, 1970.

Nemes, Sylvester. *The Soft-Hackled Fly*. Old Greenwich: Chatham Press, 1975.

Ovington, Ray. *Tactics on Trout*. New York: Alfred A. Knopf, 1969.

Rosborough, E. H. *Tying and Fishing the Fuzzy Nymphs*. 4th ed. Harrisburg: Stackpole Books, 1988.

Schwiebert, Ernest. *Trout.* New York: E. P. Dutton, 1978.

Swisher, Doug, and Carl Richards. *Fly Fishing Strategy.* New York: Crown, 1971.

Stewart, W. C. *The Practical Angler.* Edinburgh: A. & C. Black, 1857.

Willers, W. B. *Trout Biology.* Madison: The University of Wisconsin Press, 1981.

Index

About the Author

Dave Hughes is a regular contributor to *Fly Fisherman, Rod & Reel, Flyfishing, Outdoor Life,* and *Field & Stream* magazines. He is an amateur entomologist and professional writer as well as a widely traveled fly fisher. A recipient of the Lew Jewett Memorial Life Membership Award from the Federation of Fly Fishers, he is the author of *An Angler's Astoria, American Fly Tying Manual, The Complete Book of Western Hatches* (with Rick Hafele), and *Handbook of Hatches,* also from Stackpole Books.